FATHER VERNON

and

HIS CRITICS

By G. J. MacGillivray, M.A.

Fisher House, Cambridge

A Reply to "One God and Father of All"

BURNS OATES AND WASHBOURNE

FATHER VERNON

AND

HIS CRITICS

BY

G. J. MACGILLIVRAY, M.A.

Fisher House, Cambridge.

LONDON
BURNS OATES & WASHBOURNE LTD.

NIHIL OBSTAT:

GEORGIUS D. SMITH, S.T.D.

Censor deputatus.

IMPRIMATUR:

EDM. CAN. SURMONT,

Vicarius generalis.

WESTMONASTERII,

die 15 *Maji,* 1930.

First published 1930

Made and printed in Great Britain

PREFACE

WHEN Mr. Vernon Johnson, widely known
in his Anglican days as " Father Vernon,"
was received into the Catholic Church, it was
natural that he should be overwhelmed by letters
of enquiry from a host of friends who, as he puts
it, " have loved and trusted me so wonderfully,
and who are so completely at a loss to understand
why I have acted as I have." It seems also
natural that, for the satisfaction of those friends,
he should write some account of the reasons which
led him to act as he did. He accordingly did so
in a very beautiful little book entitled "One
Lord, One Faith." The book was nothing but
what it professed to be, " in no sense a polemic,
covering all possible arguments for and against,
but just a very simple account of those particular
events and reasons which led [him] to take this
step."

It is a pity that such a narrative could not be
simply taken for what it was. It was, as he says,

" in no sense a polemic." It was not an attack
on anybody, but merely a personal explanation.
It did not seem to call for any " reply." Unfortunately, however, two of his former friends
thought otherwise. In a very short time there
appeared a " reply " by Mr. Milner-White and
Mr. Wilfred Knox under the title of " One God
and Father of All." And, still more unfortunately,
this reply is distinctly polemical. It is an attack
on the Catholic Church. I do not blame them for
this attack. If they are honestly convinced, as
they obviously must be, that the Catholic
Church is such as they depict it, they are quite
right in warning their Anglican brethren against
following the example of Mr. Vernon Johnson.
But such an attack emphatically does call for a
reply. For, with the best of intentions, Mr.
Milner-White and Mr. Knox have gravely mis-
represented the Catholic Church. They do not
appear to understand her, her claims or her
teaching.

And all the more does this book call for a
reply because of the claims that have been made
for it. Mr. Morse-Boycott went so far as to say
that it " will conclude within the Anglican
Communion the Roman argument altogether.
This may sound sweeping, but it is not really.
It will end, I think, for several generations, the

tide of converts to Rome." No Catholic, of course, will fear such a result as that. It will take a great deal more than this to stop the "tide of converts." But still the book has a certain plausibility, and, if not answered, it may quite well mislead some earnest seekers after truth, and hinder them from recognising the one divinely appointed teacher of truth. That is a result which we, who believe the Catholic Church to be the one true Church of God, the one Ark of Salvation, must necessarily deplore. We cannot be content to see others deterred from sharing with us the treasures that we have found, without an effort to remove misunderstandings.

Another reason why it seems desirable that this book should be commented on from the Catholic point of view is that it shows very clearly what has been becoming increasingly evident for some time, that even the "Anglo-Catholic" party in the Church of England is rapidly drifting into Modernism. In other words, it is drifting away from any coherent Christian belief, based on reason and faith, into a sort of vague subjectivism. The writers of this book have really abandoned, as we shall see, all the old High Church positions, and appear to have no reasonable basis left for their beliefs. It is only an act of charity to point this out. For it means that the Church of England as a whole is all drifting in one direction—a drift that can only end in a complete dissolution of all definite Christian belief. It is time that those who value the historic Faith, and wish to preserve it, should see whither their leaders are carrying them, come boldly out, and return to that Church, in which alone there is stability, security and unchanging truth. If they really wish to see England return to the Catholic Faith, or indeed retain any definite faith at all, let them join forces with the only Church which keeps that Faith, the only Church which can give it once more to England.

G. J. MACGILLIVRAY.

FISHER HOUSE, CAMBRIDGE.

April 10, 1930.

CONTENTS

INTRODUCTION

ANGLO-CATHOLIC MODERNISM

THE real importance of " One God and Father of All " is that it shows very clearly the drift of the " Anglo-Catholic " party into Modernism and Rationalism, or rather something worse than Rationalism, for it is on neither faith nor reason that they now base their doctrines, but on mere irrational feeling.

" Anglo-Catholics " are very fond of talking about the great progress of the " Catholic Movement " in the Church of England since the days of Newman, Pusey and Keble. " Compare Ecclesia Anglicana seventy years ago and to-day," say Messrs. Milner-White and Knox. " The change beggars description. And it is all a Catholic change." " Anglo-Catholics " often say that such is the change that if Newman had lived to-day and seen it he would never have " gone over to Rome." But anyone who has even a slight acquaintance with Newman's writings must conclude that the very opposite is true. If

Newman had lived to-day and seen what has been
the issue of the Oxford Movement, and how the
" Anglo-Catholics " of to-day have abandoned
all the principles of that Movement, he would
have " gone over to Rome " much sooner than
he did.

Let us go to the *Apologia*. Writing of his fundamental principles and the fundamental principles of the Oxford Movement, he says : " First
was the principle of dogma : my battle was with
liberalism ; by liberalism I mean the anti-
dogmatic principle and its developments. This
was the first point on which I was certain. . . .
From the age of fifteen dogma has been the fundamental principle of my religion ; I know no other
religion ; I cannot enter into the idea of any
other sort of religion ; religion as a mere sentiment is to me a dream and a mockery. . . . Such
was the fundamental principle of the Movement
of 1833."

It was to find a definite basis for dogma, without surrendering to Rome, that the Tractarians
went back to what they called the " Primitive
Church." They believed that a definite body of
truth had been revealed by God, that it was all
contained in the Bible, but that there must be a
teaching Church with authority to interpret the
Bible.

What made Newman " go over to Rome " was that later on he saw the fallacy of looking only to the Primitive Church as the authoritative teacher. He realised that, if our Lord founded a Church to teach, that Church must go on teaching, and therefore it was not to antiquity, but to the existing Church that we must look to find the authoritative teacher. This is made quite clear in a letter, quoted in the *Apologia*, which he wrote soon after his conversion to Mr. Wilkes, the Editor of the *Christian Observer:* " If I must specify what I mean by ' Anglican Principles,' I should say, e.g., taking *Antiquity*, not the *existing Church*, as the oracle of truth ; and holding that the Apostolical Succession is a sufficient guarantee of Sacramental Grace, without union with the Christian Church throughout the world. I think these still the firmest, strongest ground against Rome—that is, *if they can be held*. They *have* been held by many, and are far more difficult to refute in the Roman controversy than those of any other religious body. For myself, I found I *could not* hold them. I left them. From the time I began to suspect their unsoundness, I ceased to put them forward. When I was fairly sure of their unsoundness, I gave up my living. When I was fully confident that the Church of Rome was the only true Church, I joined her."

The later "Anglo-Catholics" saw the difficulty. They had appealed to the Primitive
Church. But when did the Primitive Church
come to an end ? Did the Holy Ghost leave the
Church at some particular date ? And again, it
was a matter of great difficulty to find out exactly
what was the teaching of the Primitive Church.
It was still an affair of investigating and interpreting ancient documents, and if disputes about
their meaning arose, there was nobody to decide
who was right.

Then some said that you could appeal to the
early General Councils. They represented the
authentic voice of the Church. But how many
of the Councils ? Some said four, and some six.
But why did the Holy Ghost guide four or six
Councils, and not seven or eight or twenty ?

Next came the theory of the Undivided Church.
The Church could be trusted until it became
divided, which happened when Photius and his
followers broke away. But why was the Church
divided by Photius, and not by Arius or Nestorius
or Eutyches ? And again, why did the Holy
Ghost leave the Church in consequence of the
schism of Photius ? And there is still the awk-
ward difficulty that you are left with a Church
which has been silent for many centuries.

And so they took refuge in the theory that the Church is not silent, because its living voice is still to be found in the doctrines on which the "three Branches" agree. Still there are many difficulties. Who can tell what the Church of England agrees to? And if, to find the authentic teaching of the Church, you have to make for yourself a selection of doctrines on which the the three "Branches" are agreed, who can say that there is a living teaching Church, whose voice to-day is clear? And then why do these three branches alone form the Church? What about the twigs? Why are the other Protestant bodies not part of the Church? The answer was that they have no Bishops. But who said that the possession of Bishops is the one differentiating mark between bodies that are true branches and those that are not? And if that is the test, what about the Nestorians and Monophysites? Why should we not reduce the authentic doctrines to those on which they also agree with us?

"One God and Father of All" is a plain acknowledgement that all these theories have broken down. We shall see that its authors have in fact devised yet another theory. They have made a last desperate attempt to find a theory of a Church that will embrace such heterogeneous bodies as the Roman Catholic, the Eastern

" Orthodox " and the Anglican. But we shall see that, instead of being an improvement on the others, it is far less reasonable than any of them. It is obviously a counsel of despair.

But the débâcle has gone further than that. We shall see that they have entirely abandoned the idea of any teaching Authority, in any intelligible sense of the word. And with that the whole dogmatic principle has gone, and practically all belief in a Divine Revelation in the sense of a communication to man of any truths that he could not find out by his own observation and reason. They plainly do not believe that any definite truths have been revealed by God to man. The evidence for this will be apparent in the chapters that follow. But it is still more clearly seen in an article by Mr. Wilfred Knox on " The Nature of Catholic Authority " in *Theology* for February, 1929. This article illustrates the new position of the " Anglo-Catholics " so well that it is worth while giving a few extracts.

" In the New Testament we find, not the record of a divine revelation of a system of dogmas, but the reaction of the first disciples to their belief that the Master whom they had loved and followed had risen from the dead."

" The Pauline and Johannine writings record

a development in the Christian conception of the person of Jesus and His relation to God which originated in the fact that He was *felt*[1] to be the centre of Christian worship and devotion. They are attempts to explain and justify a position which He already holds, not attempts to lay dogmatic foundations for the future development of a system of cult."

" It is very difficult to hold that Christianity can claim any objective validity as a system of religion unless it be conceded that *in some sense* [1] it has in the person of Jesus a definite revelation of God to man. The historical creeds are attempts of Catholic theology to formulate what is implied in this belief and in the consciousness of communion with God which those who accepted that belief have experienced."

In other words the whole basis of our faith is that Jesus is " *felt*[1] to be the centre of Christian worship," and somehow those who believe in Him have a " consciousness of communion with God." On that slender foundation the whole structure of Catholic theology has been built up by mere human speculation. It is nothing but an attempt to account for certain " experiences." And there is no sort of certainty about it, " for it is always conceivable that there might be some

[1] Italics are mine.

other explanation." It is quite possible that very soon the whole thing will have to be scrapped, and an entirely new theology put in its place.

Could there be any clearer proof that the principles of the Oxford Movement have been entirely abandoned ? It is useless for " Anglo-Catholics " to say that during the last hundred years there has been a tremendous change in the Church of England, and that " it is all a Catholic change." It is very far from being all a Catholic change. A much larger element in it is the drift towards Modernism. It is true that many Catholic doctrines and many Catholic practices are tolerated in the Church of England. But that is because the Church of England has more and more abandoned the claim to teach anything definite.

As long ago as 1889 Mr. Wilfrid Ward, in his " William George Ward and the Oxford Movement," wrote these remarkable words : " The great spread, then, of Catholic practices and certain Catholic doctrines has taken place at the cost of the loss of the dogmatic principle, and of the essential features of a sacramental Church. Never could one-tenth of the views of the present High Church party have been tolerated on the ground that the English Church teaches them, and that dogma is in its view a sacred and important thing. A ruling power whose spirit is that of indifferentism declares all dogma to be unimportant, and High Churchmen may hold what they like, not in virtue of any special approval on the part of the Established Church, but because that Church does not either enforce or condemn *any* doctrinal system. There has, indeed, been a triumph on the part of some of the persecuted minority of that memorable 13th of February, 1845, but it is not Pusey and Keble who have triumphed ; it is rather Stanley and Jowett."

If that was true in 1889, how much more evident it is to-day. It is Stanley and Jowett who have triumphed. It is that very principle of " liberalism," that " anti-dogmatic principle," which the Oxford Movement was intended to fight, that has triumphed completely. And, as Newman foresaw, it has gone to lengths that Stanley and Jowett never dreamed of, in abandoning all reasonable ground of belief. It would be too great a compliment to call it rationalism, for it is the abandonment of reason, and an irrational reliance on mere subjective feeling. The only test of truth, according to this newest school, is what " Catholic devotion " *feels* to be true.

Messrs. Milner-White and Knox describe Modernism, which they profess to dislike, in these words : " Modernism within the Church to-day is an over-eager, muddled, unsympathetic, but honest attempt to help doubters and to be up to date in the reconciliation to which we have alluded (i.e., between the ancient Faith and " Modern Thought ") ; and suffers from not knowing thoroughly either the Faith which it re-interprets, or the science at whose heels it runs, or the needs of the souls which it is trying to help." They could hardlye have givn a better description of their own efforts. They and the avowed Modernists may have arrived at different conclusions on many points, but their principles are the same.

CHAPTER I

THE CATHOLIC CHURCH

THE difficulty in dealing with " One God and Father of All " is that there is hardly any attempt in it at reasoned argument. It begs the whole question from the start, and then proceeds by way of suggestion and appeal to sentiment rather than to reason. The authors are very skilful in the use of suggestion. To rake up all the old Protestant talk about bad Popes and the " deeds of the Inquisition," which " might shame the Soviet Government," is not serious argument, but it is effective in creating prejudice. So is the reiterated use of the phrase " oracular infallibility," and the repeated suggestion that people join the " Church of Rome " because it is an easy and comfortable escape from difficulties.

Very effective, too, is the repeated suggestion that the " Church of Rome " is narrow and uncharitable in its claim to be the one true Church of God. The very title of the book is meant to suggest this. Mr. Johnson called his book " One Lord, One Faith." Messrs. Milner-White and Knox get their title by continuing the quotation as if to say, " Ah ! yes, it is all very well to say

' One Lord, One Faith,' but have you not forgotten that higher and broader truth that there is one God and Father of all, which makes your petty exclusive claims utterly impossible ? " They say this almost in so many words. " ' One Lord, One Faith.' He could only interpret these words in a Roman sense. It is not easy to do so with those that immediately follow : ' One God and Father of All.' " And so in the Preface our authors tell us that they are " tired of this futile, barren controversy." " Can it any longer be justified as right or true or loving, or even sensible ? . . . Has this squabble on earth any meaning at all except one of pain to the larger citizenship beyond the veil ? What must God the Father of all think of it ? "

A very pretty appeal from reason to sentiment ! But note carefully what is meant by giving up controversy. It means that those tiresome Roman Catholics are to give up, without further argument, the absurd claims that they make for the Roman Church, be broad-minded, and quietly admit that Anglicans are just as much Catholics as they are. Then we shall be done with all this " futile, barren controversy " !

The authors simply assume from the outset that the Church of England is part of the Catholic Church. " Our aim," they say, " is not once

more merely to expose what we believe to be the
hopeless flaws in the *exclusive* claims of Rome
[as if that had been done already so often and so
conclusively that it is hardly worth while doing
it again]; but to suggest the valuable and unique
part which the Church of England seems called
upon to play in the economy of the whole
Catholic Church in these days of outward
division."

It is very difficult to make sense of the opening
paragraphs of Chapter I. But, if they mean
anything at all, they are a flagrant begging of the
whole question at issue. We begin with the
description of an interesting stained-glass window
in some Anglican church, in which strange
liberties are taken with the text of Holy Scripture. It " depicts the Christ giving to S John on
Patmos His message to the Angels of the Seven
Churches. Only the Churches are not Ephesus,
Smyrna, Pergamus, Thyatira, Sardis, Phila-
delphia, Laodicea, but Jerusalem (Church of
the Holy Sepulchre), Mount Athos, Venice,
Rome, Canterbury, S Paul's (London), and
Winchester. It is a parable. The Angels of three
great Christian Communions stand before the
throne of God. It is useless to say that there are
not three; there may be more; there are
certainly three—the Angel of Rome, the Angel of

Constantinople, the Angel of Canterbury. These are the Churches of the One God and Father of all ; Churches existing in order to worship Jesus Christ the Incarnate, Crucified, Risen Lord ; Churches which definitely claim unbroken descent from the Apostles through their similar ministries (a claim which history, that is to say *fact*, allows to be equally strong in each case) ; Churches which in different liturgies, but not with different purpose or meaning, celebrate the Sacraments of Jesus ; which repeat the same Creeds ; treasure the same Scriptures ; love the same Saints and Martyrs ; seek to spread the same saving Truth, to obey the same Holy Spirit of the One God and Father of all."

And then they calmly announce : " This is fact, obvious to all " ! What is fact, obvious to all ? That there exist in the world three Christian communities, of which one is in communion with Rome, another with Constantinople, and another with Canterbury ? Yes, that is obvious enough, and there are quite a number of other Christian communities, which are not in communion with any one of those sees. But hardly any of the other statements in this paragraph are obvious. It is not at all obvious that " history, that is to say fact," admits the claim of all these bodies to " unbroken descent from the

Apostles through their similar ministries." It is not obvious that they all " celebrate the Sacraments of Jesus " rightly and in their entirety, or " seek to spread the same saving Truth," since they have quite different ideas as to what the saving Truth is. In fact hardly any of the series of statements are obvious. Some of them may be true, but nearly all are open to question.

Still less obvious is the main contention, which the other statements seem designed to support, that these three communities are all " Churches of the one God and Father of all." That, in fact, is the whole question at issue. We claim that the Body, which is in communion with Rome, is the one and only " Church of the one God and Father of all." That is the very claim that this book is written to refute, and an elaborate attempt to refute it follows. Why, then, begin by stating that the falsity of the claim is " obvious to all " ? A more flagrant begging of the question can hardly be imagined.

Having, however, thus begged the main question at issue, our authors go on to attempt to prove two theses, which may be stated thus. (1) The " Church of Rome " is utterly wrong and intolerably arrogant in claiming to be the whole Catholic Church. (2) The Church of England is not only as truly a " Church of the one God and

Father of all," but a very much better one than
the "Church of Rome."

The rest of Chapter I contains the first
supposed proof of the falsity of the Roman claims.
The argument is a very ancient one—bad Popes,
the wickedness of the Inquisition—all the old
Protestant hash once more. Is it really necessary
to answer this again? Everybody knows that
there have been bad Popes, and everybody knows
that excesses were committed by some officers
of the Inquisition. These facts are very deplorable, but how do they disprove the Church's
claim? Our Lord promised that the gates of hell
would never prevail against His Church, that it
would always teach infallibly the truth revealed
by Him, and that it would always offer to all men
the means of holiness. He never promised that
all its rulers would be holy, or that none of its
officials would ever commit crimes.

But in fact this argument is put in a rather
original form. It is not intended to prove that
the Church of Rome is the " Scarlet Woman," or
the " Harlot that sitteth upon the Seven Hills,"
as the older Protestants would have said. It is
merely that these things prove that she is no
better in this respect than other churches, and
therefore cannot claim to be the one true Church.
" If Rome had been the one true infallible

Church, we should have expected its pages to be cleaner than those of its mistaken sisters. They are not. If ' the successors of S Peter ' were the divinely instituted Chief Shepherds of Christ's flock, we should have expected a line of rulers conspicuous in virtue or wisdom. It is not. As a whole it is a nobler line than any succession of secular kings can show ; but not nobler than that of the Archbishops of Canterbury."

To this one might reply in various ways. It would be easy to show that in fact the successors of S Peter have on the whole been conspicuous in both virtue and wisdom, in spite of a few unhappy exceptions. Or one might ask why they should be expected to be thus conspicuous. Our Lord never promised to endow the successors of S Peter with special virtue and wisdom. What He promised was that their faith would never fail, and that they would confirm their brethren. And that, in spite of occasional lapses in their private life, they have always done.

But in fact the comparison put in this way is absurd. The suggestion is that the " Church of Rome " and the Church of England (or should we not say the " Church of Canterbury " ?) have always existed side by side as separate entities, and that you can thus compare their records all through the ages. But, as it is manifest to every-

body who has not an " Anglo-Catholic " thesis
to maintain, until the sixteenth century the
Church in England was merely a part of the one
Catholic Church, of which the Pope was the
acknowledged head, the only possible comparison
is between these two bodies as they have existed
since then. Or, rather, the true question is
whether the Church of England has gained by
breaking away from Rome.

Now, what are the facts ? The results of the
" Reformation " were disastrous from every
point of view. The Catholic Faith was distorted
and mutilated, there was an immediate and
deplorable decline in morals, foreign missions
ceased, and the seeds were sown of most of the
social evils from which we are now suffering.

But we are asked to admire the signs that the
" persistent vitality " of the Church of England
is as great as that of the " Roman " Church.
The signs are that during the last century there
has been great activity in the matter of foreign
missions, that there has been " a revival of
specifically Catholic devotion," and that " a
stream of scholars as fine as any age of the Church
can show, building on purely Catholic foundations,
have met modern thought and criticism on their
own ground, and have been conspicuously successful in reconciling old truth and new, to the

greater fulness of each." And so we are asked
to " compare Ecclesia Anglicana seventy years
ago and to-day. The change beggars description.
And it is all a Catholic change."

What does all this mean ? It means that a
section of the Church of England has to some
extent recovered from the disastrous effects of
breaking away from Rome. The Catholic
Church has, of course, never slackened in its
zeal for foreign missions. It might have been
thought that with the great revolt of the sixteenth century its energies would have been all
absorbed in dealing with that revolt, but in fact
there never was a time when foreign missions
flourished more. The Church of England, on the
contrary, showed no concern at all about the
heathen for the first two hundred and fifty years
of its existence. That during the last hundred
years it has done something to repair that neg-
lect is certainly to its credit, but hardly a thing
to boast about. It is merely a tardy reparation.

The sentence about the stream of scholars is
wholly unintelligible. That the Church of
England has had many distinguished scholars is
true. But what is meant by saying that " building
on purely Catholic foundations, [they] have met
modern thought and criticism on their own
ground, and have been conspicuously successful

in reconciling old truth and new, to the greater fulness of each " ? Whether they built on purely Catholic foundations depends upon what you mean by Catholic. They have certainly not been Catholic in the sense in which that term is used by the world at large. Indeed, to say that they built upon a purely Catholic foundation is only another begging of the question. It can only be maintained by those who assume that the Church of England is Catholic. Whether they have been " conspicuously successful in reconciling old truth and new " is a matter of opinion. I should say that they have been conspicuously unsuccessful, and that they have merely abandoned as much of the truth revealed by God as they could not reconcile with the fashionable opinions of the day.

The chapter ends with the amazing statement that the authors " are bound to point out in this and the following chapters some of the ways in which the Church of England bears witness to Catholic faith, tradition, and life with a power that is unequalled in its sister communions." They do not seem to have done so very successfully in this chapter. It remains to be seen whether they have done so in succeeding chapters.

CHAPTER II

CATHOLIC LOVE

TO a Catholic this chapter is painful reading. We can only wonder how the authors have got their so completely mistaken idea of our attitude towards those whom we call " our separated brethren." They accuse the Catholic Church of failing in love towards them. How are we to answer this ? It does not seem to be of much use saying that the Catholic Church loves every human being in this world with a love which is that of God Himself, because they do not seem disposed to believe it. And yet that is the plain truth. Individual Catholics, of course, may fail, and do. But the Catholic Church itself is the Body of Christ—the living Organism, in which Christ dwells in the world always. Therefore its love is His love. Its one desire is the same as His, namely, to draw all human beings into union with God, to make them one with Him, and one with one another in love.

But let us see what are the grounds of this terrible accusation. " She does not," the authors say, " seek nor want to understand non-Roman positions or piety ; she will not even pray with non-Romans." " To the world outside its exclusiveness has come to be a chief mark of Roman Catholicism." " It is a condemnation without trial or sympathy, not of Christ's enemies, but of all Catholic and Christian believers who do not submit to papal jurisdiction." It is " so narrow as to exclude even the simplest courtesies of specifically Christian love." And finally the Church is invited " to make a qualified admission that, since the sin of the original division was due to faults on both sides, she cannot condemn such other bodies at least as have kept Catholic faith and order. That, though she believed them mistaken, she believed also their mistake to be honest ; and preferred to win them back to visible unity by a policy of love and friendly sympathy rather than by one of exclusion and hostile propaganda."

Now the only thing to be said about these charges is that they are entirely untrue. It is untrue that we do not " seek nor want to understand non-Roman positions or piety." We are continually trying to understand them, although sometimes it is very difficult. We do not " exclude the simplest courtesies of specifically Christian love " from anybody. We are continually saying that we believe the vast majority of non-Catholic Christians to be honest in their mistakes. And we are continually trying to win them to visible unity by a policy of love and friendly sympathy, and in fact succeeding in the case of many thousands every year.

The only statement here that has a semblance of truth is that we " will not pray with them." Even that is not really true, for in fact we are glad that they should come and join with us in prayer. What is true is that we will not join in Protestant services, or hold " undenominational " services. But that is not a want of charity, but a matter of principle.

And is there not here the clue to what really makes Mr. Milner-White and Mr. Knox accuse us of want of charity ? What really annoys them is our claim that what they call the " Roman " Church is the one true Church of God. That, and all that necessarily follows from it, is what seems to them " exclusiveness," narrowness, and want of charity.

They accuse us of not trying to understand their position. Have they really tried to understand ours ? Do they really understand that we are honestly convinced that this Church, to which we belong, is the only true Church of God ? This is not arrogance. We are not claiming any merit for ourselves. We did not make the Catholic Church. Our belief may seem to them mistaken, but at least they might try to understand that we do believe it, and to understand what the necessary consequences of such a belief are.

That they do not understand is shown by some of the phrases that they use. They talk about condemning " all Catholic and Christian believers who do not submit to papal jurisdiction," and ask us to acknowledge that we " cannot condemn such other bodies at least as have kept Catholic faith and order." But the fact is that we do not believe that there *are* any Catholic believers outside the " Roman " Church, or that any other bodies *have* kept Catholic faith and order.

If they understood this, they would also understand why we will not join in their services. It is a plain fact that all the Protestant churches were set up in opposition to the Catholic Church. Consequently, we must regard them as being in a state of rebellion against the one Church of Christ. We know that most of them are in good faith, and that their rebellion is not intentional. No doubt they honestly think that the Catholic Church has gone wrong, and that they are right in maintaining these other bodies in opposition to it. But we believe that it *is* rebellion and that their worship is set up in opposition to the worship of the true Church, and therefore we cannot join in it.

This, then, is the real trouble. We will not admit that they are just as much Catholics as we are. We will not join in their services. We will not discuss with them on equal terms, or admit that there may be mistakes on both sides, and that by means of some sort of round-table conference we might arrive at some compromise. We will insist that the " Roman " Church is infallible, and cannot compromise on any single point.

Again, therefore, I ask Mr. Milner-White and Mr. Knox to try to put themselves in our position, to imagine themselves holding the convictions that we do. We believe that the " Roman " Church is the one true Church of God, the one Ark of Salvation. We believe that God the Holy Ghost so dwells in it, and guides it, that it must always teach the truth and cannot err. We believe that all other Christian bodies have been set up in opposition to the one true Church, contrary to the will of God, and that they teach error. To us, who believe these things, what is true charity to those who unhappily belong to those other Christian bodies ? Is it to compromise, to discuss, to join in their services, as

c

if there were no essential difference between us ? No, the only true charity is to try to put the truth before them, to persuade them to leave those bodies that have been set up in opposition to the will of God, and to come and share with us the inestimable blessings of belonging to the one true Church of God.

They cannot see that it is nothing but charity, love of God and love of all God's children that makes us seek by every means to bring them into the one true Church. We are not concerned with " churches " or " communions," but with human souls. We are firmly convinced that the Holy Catholic and Roman Church is the one Ark of Salvation. We are filled with love and compassion for those unhappy souls who are wandering outside, through no fault of their own, but through the sins of their forefathers, who broke away from the Church of God. We know that it is not their fault. We know that they are honestly mistaken. We do not condemn them or blame them at all. All we want to do is to show them that they are mistaken, and to bring them back to the one Fold of Christ, for His sake and theirs. What greater charity can there be than to try to persuade others to come and share with us the priceless treasures that we have found ?

CHAPTER III

CATHOLIC TRUTH

THE next accusation against the Catholic
Church is that she takes no notice of all the
new knowledge and consequent new questions
and new criticisms of the present day. " We
live," we are told, " in an age, the intellectual
greatness of which has never been approached in
the history of the world. New revelations—no
lesser word can be used—come streaming into
the knowledge of men daily : knowledge of the
size and composition of the universe ; of the
mind of man and the capacities of the human
spirit. Historical science investigates (purely
for the sake of truth) documents and traditions
and growths, explaining, re-valuing evidence,
reconstructing the past. Philosophical thought,
with so much new material to work upon, goes
deeper and deeper into vital meanings. And to all
this splendid and beneficent energy after truth, to
all this piercing criticism, based often on incontrovertible facts, the Roman branch of the
Catholic Church has nothing to contribute,

nothing to say, except 'Here is the Catholic Faith in its sixteenth-century expression, plus the infallibility of the Pope.'"

The Church of England on the other hand, they maintain, honestly accepts all these "new revelations," "realises that the two systems of truth (both in their different measure and by different method the gift of the one God and Father of all) are in danger of standing apart, contrary to the mind of God, and to their own impoverishment, and to the world's distraction." It therefore labours to effect a reconciliation between them, "and to show to world and Church that the Catholic Faith has nothing to fear or to lose from modern science or thought, but much to gain ; and vice versa."

We are told that this was not always the case. "Up to the Reformation the Western Church took its intellectual duty to God and to the world very seriously. As new modes of thought, new philosophies of life, entered the West, it debated, discussed, drew from them their valuable truths, reconciled them with the Historic Faith, and enriched orthodoxy by inspired travail of mind."

With the Reformation, they think, came a change in the Church's attitude. Faced with that "indignant revolt," it then "took the step of suppressing all free expression of theological opinion and of critical learning." And this continues to the present day. "The Church of Rome has never recovered from the terror of the Reformation." And the result is a "blight thus thrown upon the investigations of Catholic scholarship and all progress in theological thought. And this in a day when, among educated and candid people, the truth cannot hope to be recognised as truth unless it can be verified and defended by the instrument which God has given for that purpose, the intellect of man."

To one who knows both the Church of England and the Catholic Church from inside all this is simply bewildering. Perhaps it is most easily answered by a personal experience. I was for many years a member and a clergyman of the Church of England. I began to study theology at Cambridge, and continued to do so as well as I could on the lines that I learned to follow there. I need not here describe how, bewildered by conflicting voices, I searched for truth, and at last found it in the Catholic Church. Having been received into the Church, and finding a vocation to the Priesthood, I went to begin the study of theology anew at the Gregorian University in Rome. Did I there find my intellect and reason stifled? Exactly the opposite. I

can never forget what was my dominant thought
when I entered on my studies there. I was continually saying to myself, "Thank God, now
at last I am allowed to use my reason!" After
all these years of being told that "you must not
be too logical," of evasions of vital issues, of
talk about feelings and experiences, and of
contradictory statements being "different as-
pects of truth," what a relief to sit and listen to
clearly thought out, logical arguments! And
yet we are told that the Catholic Church stifles
reason!

But really is not this accusation a little out of
date? One would have thought that it was
fairly obvious by this time that the only Church
which fearlessly follows reason in theological
matters is the Catholic Church. Everywhere else
there is a strange distrust of reason. It is nowhere more evident than in "One God and
Father of All."

And then to talk about the "blight thrown
upon the investigations of Catholic scholarship
and all progress in theological thought!" One
can only suppose that Mr. Milner-White and
Mr. Knox are entirely ignorant of all Catholic
theology since the sixteenth century. Have they
never heard of John of St. Thomas, Gonet, the
Salmanticenses, Suarez, De Lugo, Billuart,

Franzelin, Hürter, Billot, Zigliara, Janssens, Gardeil, Garrigou-Lagrange, Maritain—to mention a few names out of many which immediately come to mind ? The fact is that it is only in the Catholic Church that there is any progress in theological thought. There is real progress, because we go on steadily from truth already acquired to further investigations. Outside the Catholic Church there is no progress, because nothing is certain, everything is chaos. To abandon truth long since acquired, and to take up one new theory after another is not progress, for it leads nowhere.

The attitude of the Catholic Church to " new modes of thought " and " new philosophies of life " has not changed since the Reformation. It is to-day the same as it always has been. It investigates, weighs and considers them all with the utmost care, assimilating what is true and rejecting what is false. It does not swallow them all wholesale, assuming that the latest new theory or the latest new philosophy must be right. It never did that. There were quite a number of philosophies in the Middle Ages, such as Averroism and Nominalism, for example, which the Church knew very well and deliberately rejected. Its attitude is the same to-day. It is quite ready to welcome any new philosophical ideas that can be reconciled with truth already known, and especially with the truth revealed by God, which is the Catholic Faith. And if it rejects most of the fashionable philosophies of to-day it is because it has examined them and decided that they cannot be reconciled with that Faith, and are untrue.

Our authors entirely mistake the functions and effects of the Censorship and the Index. They are no check, much less a " blight," on the investigations of scholars and theologians. They merely protect the Faithful from being led astray. To place a book on the Index is equivalent to labelling it " Poison." It is a warning to the unlearned that it contains false doctrines, and that they ought to avoid reading it, or they will have their minds poisoned with untruth. Of course scholars and theologians, whose studies make it necessary for them to be acquainted with such books, have no difficulty in obtaining permission to read them. The Censorship has a similar purpose. An " imprimatur " is a guarantee that, in the opinion of the competent theologian who acts as censor, the book bearing it contains nothing contrary to faith or morals. Surely this also is a much needed safeguard ; without some such system the unlearned would never know what books they could trust.

These precautions do not hinder investigation. Scholars and theologians are free to investigate as much as they like. Only there is a check upon their publishing anything that is likely to lead the unlearned astray.

The real difference between theological research inside and outside the Catholic Church is that in the Catholic Church we have a criterion by which to judge new ideas. Investigators outside have no such criterion. For them nothing is certain. They are liable at any moment to throw overboard the most venerable beliefs in favour of the latest new fashionable theory, and that is in fact what they often do. But they have no guarantee that the latest theory is true, or will not in its turn be abandoned in favour of something newer still. The Catholic Church, on the other hand, knows that whatever has up to now been defined is true. It has a definite body of ascertained truth, by their conformity or want of conformity with which all new theories must be judged. Consequently it is able to follow S Paul's maxim : " Prove all things, hold fast that which is good."

Our authors come nearer to the facts when they say : " The Church of Rome interprets Catholic Truth as something different from, and un-affected by, the advance of knowledge and the progress of scholarship." In a sense this is true. Catholic Truth is the Truth revealed by God, and cannot be changed by any advance in knowledge. New knowledge may throw new light upon it, illustrate it, make its implications clearer, and so forth. But certainly no new knowledge can make any essential difference to it. It cannot and it has not. No new knowledge has produced any demonstrated fact which conflicts with any dogma defined by the Church.

And here it is necessary to insist again on the difference between newly acquired knowledge of facts and new theories. There are plenty of modern theories which are in conflict with the Church's teaching, but theories are very different from ascertained facts. And it is simply true that nobody can mention a single ascertained *fact* which conflicts with any Catholic dogma.

This is followed by a particularly plausible but essentially misleading paragraph : " The Historic Faith must be expressed in the terms of some age. Rome presents the Historic Faith (on the whole) in the light of sixteenth-century thought (at latest). Canterbury presents the Historic Faith (on the whole) in the light of modern thought. We can add, if we like, that Constantinople presents the Historic Faith in terms of, say, eighth-century thought. If you want and trust anti-

quity of presentation—which is a tenable desire
—go to Constantinople. If you believe that the
best thought of our age can contribute to the
riches of the Catholic Faith, go to Canterbury.
Rome provides a *via media*."

The implication is that the Eastern Church
stopped thinking and working out the meaning
of the Faith about the eighth century, and that
the " Roman " Church did the same in the
sixteenth, while only the Anglican Church continues a vigorous intellectual life, bringing forth
out of its treasure " things new and old." With
regard to the Eastern Church, that is roughly
true. Since its separation from Rome it has
been intellectually sterile, merely going on repeat-
ing the formulæ of the first seven General
Councils. But to suggest that since the sixteenth century the Anglican Church has done all
the thinking, while " Rome " has been sterile,
merely shows colossal ignorance of Catholic
theological work of the last four centuries.

The fact is that the Catholic Church simply
goes on with its steady progress. It does not
want to go back and " re-state " what has already
been adequately stated, whether in the fourth
century, or in the thirteenth or in the sixteenth.
Whatever has been worked out in past ages it
keeps. The Church in the thirteenth century did

not discard the definitions of the fourth or fifth, nor did it in the sixteenth century discard those of the thirteenth. It merely developed the implications of the Faith further, sometimes making new definitions, sometimes even inventing new terms, when such were required, but not abandoning the old. Exactly the same process has been going on since then, and will go on.

What " Canterbury " does is to put the whole thing continually back into the melting pot, whenever it gets a new idea from the latest fashionable philosophy. They call that progress, but it is the very reverse. You do not progress on a journey when you are constantly running back to your starting point to see whether you have not somewhere taken a wrong turning.

What, then, is to be said of this remarkable claim : " We have only to look at the Church of England with unprejudiced eye to see that, despite these partial and vociferous modernisms, the full light of the Historic Faith only waxes brighter and brighter. Compare her conscious and comprehended Catholicism now with that of a hundred years ago, sixty years ago, thirty years ago, ten years ago. A robust and clear-sighted faith has grounds for arguing that Modernism, whether Anglican or foreign, has been over-ruled conspicuously for good."

I have already, in my introductory chapter, quoted specimens of " Anglo-Catholic " Modernism from Mr. Wilfred Knox's article in *Theology*. Other examples may be found in a volume entitled " Essays Catholic and Critical," which appeared three or four years ago, compiled by a number of leaders of the " Anglo-Catholic " party. There we have Dr. E. O. James solemnly giving out some of the wildest theories about the origin of religion, as if they were definitely ascertained facts, instead of being, as they are, merely the speculations of a certain school of anthropologists. Mr. Rawlinson and Mr. Wilfred Knox are thoroughly modernistic in their conception of Authority, practically resolving it all into the " Interpretation of Experience," in the best manner of Loisy, Tyrrell, and the rest. Mr. Bicknell entirely abandons the Catholic doctrine of the Fall and Original Sin, thus making nonsense of the whole scheme of Christianity. And we shall find some more startling examples in later chapters of this book, but we have already enough to enable us to judge of this astonishing claim.

The only way in which Modernism in the Anglican Church can be said to have been over-ruled for good is that the issue is becoming clearer. The idea of the Church of England as

a whole being gradually brought back to the
Faith by the influence of the " Anglo-Catholics "
is seen more clearly than ever to be an empty
dream, since the leaders of the party have themselves surrendered to Modernism.   The issue
hereafter is between the one Holy, Catholic and
Roman Church on the one hand, and Modernism
in all its varying forms on the other.

CHAPTER IV

S TERESA OF LISIEUX

"THE argument from S Teresa of Lisieux," our authors say, "proves nothing except as against that tiny minority of Protestants which really believes that Rome is Antichrist and the Scarlet Woman of the Apocalypse." But can Chapters II and III of Mr. Johnson's book be properly described as an "argument" at all? Are they intended to be an argument? I should say not. It is just a very charming and straightforward narrative of how he was led to the conviction that the "Roman" Church is the one true Church of God. His experience at Lisieux was simply the starting point.

In S Teresa, he says, he discovered a heroic sanctity, a "miracle of supernatural grace," such as he had never met before. He was forced to ask himself why he "had never met anything like it in the Church of England." That started him on his enquiry. It made him begin to examine the claims of the "Roman" Church as he had never done before. He examined them, and found them to be justified. It is in later chapters that he gives us a sketch of the arguments that finally convinced him.

"Yes," his critics would reply, "but the starting point was wrong. He ought not to have been so exceptionally impressed by S Teresa, because there are just as great Saints in the Church of England." Mr. Johnson says that he had "never seen anything like it in the Church of England." I can only answer his critics by saying that my experience is the same. I have met many very good people in the Church of England, but I have certainly never seen or heard of anything like the sanctity of S Teresa, or of any other Catholic Saint. It is not an easy thing to argue about. People must judge for themselves. Let them read the lives of some of our Saints—S Philip Neri, S Francis Xavier, S Charles Borromeo, the Curé d'Ars, S Teresa of the Child Jesus—and answer the question for themselves, whether the Church of England, from its foundation in the sixteenth century until now, has produced such characters as these. Mr. Johnson tells us that he had not discovered them. I can only add that I have not discovered them either. Consequently, Mr. Johnson was perfectly right in asking himself why it is that the Catholic Church alone can produce Saints, and was wise in pursuing the enquiry.

That is the first answer to our authors'
challenge : " It is for Romans, not for Anglicans,
to explain how it is that the grace of God is
diffused so far beyond the limits of the one true
Church." Grace, in the measure that produces
Saints, does not extend beyond the limits of the
one true Church.

If, however, it is a question of the more
ordinary degrees of grace—that which is necessary
for salvation, or such as produces really good and
holy people, though falling short of being Saints
in the full sense—the answer is simply to be
found in the infinite goodness of God. The
Catholic Church is the one channel of grace
appointed by God, but such is His goodness
that His grace overflows its appointed channel
to all those who, through no fault of their own,
are ignorant of, or fail to discover, the appointed
channel, or are, as we say, in " invincible
ignorance."

Messrs. Milner-White and Knox indignantly
scoff at this doctrine of invincible ignorance.
They tell us that many good men, " perfectly
qualified to judge of the truth or falsehood of
the arguments," and who have studied them
thoroughly, have nevertheless rejected them.
They forget that the acceptance of supernatural
truth is not a mere question of argument. The

arguments for the truth of the Catholic claims
are abundant, but they do not compel assent, as
a mathematical demonstration does. The will
has a good deal to do with it, and so has grace.
Faith is a gift of God. It presupposes reason,
but reason alone will not produce faith. It
needs also the grace of God to enlighten the
understanding and to move the will. And why
God gives the grace to recognise the true Church
to one person and not to another is a mystery of
His Providence, which nobody in this world can
solve.

It is a little difficult to take seriously the argument that, because we now know the material
universe to be much larger than the early
Christians thought it to be, we can no longer
believe that God is "so keenly interested in
questions of ecclesiastical organisation, however
important."

One might easily retort : " Then why make
such a fuss about your supposed 'historic
episcopate'"? Or one might ask how any
question can be "important" that is of little
interest to God.

But in fact it is not a "question of ecclesiastical organisation." It is the question whether
God has formed a particular Body, a particular
living Organism (for that is what the Catholic

Church really is), to be the one appointed channel
to convey supernatural grace to men. And
what the size and duration of the material universe has to do with that it passes the wildest
efforts of my imagination to conceive. It
reminds one of the argument of a certain type
of very shallow unbeliever, who argues against
the Incarnation on the ground that, since this
planet is such a tiny speck in the vastness of
space, it is inconceivable that God should have
selected it for such a special favour. But it is
not usual to address such arguments to intelli-
gent people.

Lastly we come to " the old test of the Gospels,
' by their fruits ye shall know them.' " By that
saying of our Divine Lord we are quite content
that the Catholic Church should be judged. The
question, however, is not whether particular
converts to the Church necessarily show a
marked progress in holiness, although in fact
the majority of them do. But the question is
rather whether the Catholic Church as a whole
shows more abundant fruits of holiness than the
Church of England. Those of us who have known
both from the inside unhesitatingly answer
" Yes."

It is curious, by the way, how Mr. Milner-
White and Mr. Knox calmly assert that these

fruits are more abundant in bodies that have " the use of the Sacraments in communion with the historic episcopate " than in others. As they believe themselves to have the " historic episcopate," this means that the fruits of holiness are more abundant among Anglicans, "Orthodox" Greeks, Monophysites, Nestorians and so forth, than among any of the non-episcopal bodies. I have certainly not noticed it. I should say that Wesleyans, Scottish Presbyterians and Quakers can show quite as much holiness as Anglicans, and considerably more than most of those Eastern Churches with which I happen to have some personal acquaintance.

The Catholic Church, however, is quite another matter. The Church of England produces numbers of excellent and respectable citizens, and also a good proportion of really holy people. Nobody wants to deny that. But for the production of the distinctively supernatural virtues in abundance it is to the Catholic Church that you must go. Nobody, who knows both from inside, can possibly doubt that.

CHAPTER V

AUTHORITY IN THE NEW TESTAMENT

BY his experience at Lisieux Mr. Johnson was impelled to examine seriously the claims of the " Roman " Church, and, naturally enough, he betook himself to a fresh study of the New Testament. In the following chapters of this book he gives in a very simple and straightforward way the results.

At Lisieux he had discovered a Church which, unlike the Church of England, spoke with authority, being quite confident that it had received power from our Lord to teach in His name, and that He had promised so to guide it that it would always teach without error the truth revealed by Him. Therefore he turned to his New Testament to find out whether that was the kind of Church that our Lord founded, and whether He really did give it such authority. In Chapters IV to IX he gives us the results of his researches. With a wealth of quotations he proves quite clearly the following facts :—

1. Our Lord claimed to speak with authority.

He claimed to have come into the world to reveal to men the truth about God, our relation to God, and the way to eternal life.

2. He gave to the Church, which He founded, authority to teach in His name. It was to be " the shrine of His own authority." It was to continue His work, to teach with the same authority that He had. And He promised that He would be with it always, to enable it to fulfil that task, and to preserve it from all error.

3. In the Acts and Epistles we find the Church teaching with authority, teaching a definite body of truth as revealed by God, conscious of divine authority, and demanding obedience and submission.

And then he points out that the only Church which claims such authority to-day, and teaches in that way, is the " Roman " Church.

The argument is very well set out, supported by abundance of texts from Holy Scripture, sufficient to convince any unprejudiced person.

Now let us see how Messrs. Milner-White and Knox deal with this argument. Their answer may be summarised under four propositions :—

1. Mr. Johnson " accepts the literal accuracy and truth of every word of the Authorised Version with the absolute conviction of those who, since the famous trial in Tennessee, are known

to all the world as ' Fundamentalists.' "   But in
fact a considerable part of the New Testament is
quite unreliable.

2. " The only thing which our long arrays of
texts will give is the simple point that our Lord
claimed to teach with authority, that He gave
His disciples authority to preach in His name,
and that He intended them to do so through a
visible society."   But our Lord's promises were
" dependent on the perseverance of His followers."   He promised to them the guidance of
the Holy Spirit to lead them into all truth, " but
this guidance depends not on their acceptance of
the authority of the Church, but on their
loyalty to the example and the Spirit of the Lord
Himself."

3. That our Lord's promises did not imply an
" oracular infallibility " is proved by the fact
that from the beginning the Church had no
definite teaching.   At first it did not even teach
the fundamental truth of our Lord's Divinity.
Indeed, our Lord Himself did not claim to be
God.   " It was only by degrees that the Church
came to see that the position of our Lord in His
own teaching, and in the life and worship of the
Church, implied the belief that He was God."

4. That the Church had no " oracular infallibility " is further proved by the fact that the

Apostles themselves made a grave mistake. " If the teaching of the Apostles was clear and definite about any single point, it was the imminence of the Second Coming of our Lord to judge both the quick and the dead." But on this point they were clearly mistaken, seeing that He has not come yet. Therefore they had no " oracular infallibility."

With these objections I must proceed to deal in order.

1. I find no evidence in Mr. Johnson's book that he accepts the literal accuracy and truth of every word of the " Authorised Version," after the manner of the " Fundamentalists " of Tennessee. All that is required for his argument is that in the four Gospels we have a *substantially* accurate account of what our Lord did and taught. (I am not here dealing with the Catholic doctrine of Inspiration, but with what is required for Mr. Johnson's argument.) And in spite of nearly a century of destructive criticism, mostly German, it has been demonstrated over and over again that this is the case. The numerous scholars who have defended the Gospels are quite as competent as those who have attacked them.

Naturally, in a book of this kind, which was never intended to be a complete apologetic treatise, but a simple narrative of the mental process that led to his conversion, he could not answer all the theories of the critics, and prove over again the reliability of the Gospels.

Messrs. Milner-White and Knox complain that, because of this acceptance of the Gospel narratives as they stand, " it is a little difficult to know where to begin." It is clear that they ought to have begun by telling us how much of the Gospels they accept. They brush aside the Fourth Gospel, and they reject the conclusion of the Second. But that does not take us very far. Are we permitted to accept the rest of the Synoptic Gospels as substantially accurate ? Or can we rely only on Mark (or perhaps a lost " Ur-Marcus "), and " Q " ?

I wonder whether Mr. Milner-White and Mr. Knox realise the mischievous effect of writing in this way, and that not so much by what they definitely say, as by what they suggest. They actually only say that Mr. Johnson is wrong in his supposed acceptance of " the literal accuracy and truth of every word of the Authorised Version," that " it is generally admitted by the most orthodox scholars that the Fourth Gospel cannot be pressed as containing the actual words of our Lord, but rather an interpretation of His Person by a disciple in the light of half a century

or so of Christian experience," and that the
conclusion of S Mark's Gospel "was added to
that Gospel at a later date, after the original
conclusion had been lost." But the general
impression they will leave on the unlearned is
that the Gospels are very unreliable, and that
nothing much can be built upon them.

They apparently wish to imply that everyone
who does not accept all the alleged "results" of
the destructive German critics must be classed
with those curious Protestants of Tennessee,
who insist on the literal interpretation of everything in the Bible. They apparently wish to
give the impression that the attitude of Catholics
to the Bible is the same as that of the prosecutors
in the Dayton case. And yet they ought to
know that nothing is further from the truth.
The Catholic Church has never held that the
whole Bible is to be interpreted literally. But
the acceptance of all the wildest speculations of
the German critics is not the only alternative to
that.

It is not quite clear what our authors mean
by their curious description of the Fourth Gospel.
Nobody supposes that S John took down our
Lord's discourses in shorthand, and reproduced
them word for word. But what is meant by
calling it "an interpretation of His Person by

a disciple in the light of half a century or so of Christian experience "? If it means anything at all, it means that it is pure fiction, that it does not represent what our Lord taught, but what " a disciple," who had long afterwards come to the conclusion that He was God, thought that He ought to have taught. That is in fact the view of many rationalistic German critics and their English admirers. But to say that it is " generally admitted by the most orthodox scholars " is simply not true. The historicity and the Johannine authorship of the Fourth Gospel have been defended over and over again by arguments that cannot be refuted. And still more has the general accuracy of the account given of our Lord's life and teaching in the four Gospels been vindicated repeatedly. (Those who wish to read an exhaustive treatment of the whole subject should consult " Christ and the Critics," by Hilarin Felder.)

2. However, having thus thrown doubt on the value of the texts quoted by Mr. Johnson, our authors go on to argue that in any case they do not prove what he seeks to prove. " The only thing," they say, " which our long arrays of texts will give is the simple point that our Lord claimed to teach with authority, that He gave His disciples authority to teach in His Name,

and that He intended them to do so through a visible society. It may be admitted that the texts prove this, but unfortunately they prove nothing to which the extremest of Protestants would for a moment hesitate to subscribe. We go on to the Church in the Acts and Epistles. Here again our texts prove nothing that any Protestant would hesitate to accept, for they simply prove that the Church is, in the New Testament, and ought to be at present, the sacramental expression of the indwelling power of the Holy Ghost, preserving its teaching from error and guiding them into truth." And again, at the end of the chapter, it is admitted that our Lord promised to His followers the guidance of the Holy Ghost to lead them to the truth, "but this guidance depends not on their acceptance of the authority of the Church, but on their loyalty to the example and the Spirit of the Lord Himself."

In spite of some curious expressions, the general meaning of this is clear enough. Our Lord gave no real authority to His Church at all. He made no promise that He would so guide His Church that it would continue, even for a few years, to teach the truth revealed by Him—if, indeed, He did reveal any truth at all. He made no such promise even to the Apostles. The promise is merely that such individual Christians as are loyal to His example and to His Spirit will be guided into truth. The whole idea of a teaching Church is abandoned. The sense attached to these promises by " the extremest of Protestants " is right.

Of course this is a complete abandonment of the position taken up by the " Anglo-Catholic " party from the days of the Oxford Movement until now. The old High Churchmen thought that at least they could appeal to what they called the " Primitive Church." Clearly that can no longer be done. It is a reversion to the purest Protestantism, except that the old Protestants thought that they had an infallible authority in the Bible, and these new " Anglo-Catholic " Protestants do not even believe that.

But now I would ask any candid person to read again the texts quoted by Mr. Johnson, and ask himself whether that is all that they mean. It is useless to go over the ground here again, for Mr. Johnson has done it very well. He has shown quite clearly that our Lord founded a definite Teaching Body, and to that Body He promised that He would so guide it that it would be able always to teach with His own authority. He would so guide it that it would always teach the truth revealed by Him. And then in the

Acts and Epistles we find that Body conscious of its authority, teaching a definite body of truth as revealed by God, and demanding submission and obedience.

I find nowhere in the Gospels that the promise was merely made to such individuals as were loyal to His example and His Spirit, and that individuals who considered themselves to be thus loyal could be sure of such guidance without submission to the Teaching Body. Nor do I find any hint that such ideas were tolerated in the Apostolic Church. There were such people, but S Paul bluntly says of them : " A man that is an heretic ($\alpha\iota\rho\epsilon\tau\iota\kappa\delta s$ = one who chooses a way of his own, instead of accepting the authoritative teaching of the Church) after the first and second admonition reject."

But we are told that our Lord's promises could not have implied an " oracular infallibility," that is, any infallibility at all, because from the beginning the Church had no definite teaching. At first it did not even teach the fundamental truth of our Lord's Divinity. Mr. Johnson, we are told, shows crass ignorance when he quotes from the Girton Conference the sentence, " Christ did not claim divinity for Himself," as a specimen of Modernism. " It was only by degrees that the Church came to see that the position of our

Lord in His own teaching and in the life and worship of the Church implied the belief that He was God. We see S Paul working steadily to this conclusion when he writes of our Lord in Colossians as " the image of the invisible God," " the first-born of all creation," or again when he says in Philippians that our Lord, " being in the form of God, thought it not an object of ambition to be made equal to God." (A bad translation, as I shall show presently.) It is only in the Fourth Gospel, one of the latest writings of the New Testament, that we come to the triumphant conclusion, " The Word was God."

What all this amounts to is that belief in our Lord's Divinity was just an idea, at which Christians arrived after many years. At first (according to this theory) they thought of Him only as a human Messiah. Then, as devotion grew, and (as Mr. Knox puts it in the article in *Theology*, from which I have already quoted) " He was *felt*[1] to be the centre of Christian worship and devotion," they gradually exalted Him higher and higher, until at last after fifty years or so they came to think of Him as actually God, and then " a disciple " wrote a new Gospel, in which with flagrant dishonesty he puts into our Lord's mouth claims that He never made.

[1] Italics are mine.

Now, we have read this kind of thing over and over again in a whole array of rationalistic German critics, from F. C. Baur and Strauss down to Wrede and Schweitzer. The astounding thing is to find these theories advanced by people who loudly proclaim that they are Catholics, and that they hold the same faith as we do. Not only do they not hold the same faith as we do, but they are immeasurably further removed from us, and from the whole Catholic tradition of 1900 years than the old-fashioned High Churchmen of fifty or eighty years ago, and even than the old Evangelicals. *They* differed from us in very important matters, but this new school of " Anglo-Catholics " have simply abandoned the foundations. It is no longer a question of the number of the sacraments and so forth, but of the fact of a Divine Revelation in any intelligible sense at all. They may have come to different conclusions from the Girton Conference people on certain matters, but fundamentally their position is the same. The whole belief in a Divine Revelation, as that has been understood by all Christians for 1900 years, has been abandoned. For them there is no such thing as a " Faith once delivered to the Saints." It is all human speculation, and not even founded on reason, but on feeling and sentiment.

This is all very sad, because, instead of leading their followers on to the Catholic Faith, these " Anglo-Catholic " clergymen are merely leading them into the quagmire of rationalism and infidelity. Sooner or later they will begin to think for themselves, and the danger is that seeing the unstable foundation on which their belief rested, they will abandon it all without having anything better with which to replace it. And still more disastrous is the effect likely to be on those who have no very definite belief, but are feeling their way towards one. This sort of thing, if they come across it, will merely confirm them in unbelief. They will naturally think that, if that is the best that can be made of Christianity, there is not much to be said for it.

But are these clergymen right in thus accepting wholesale the destructive criticism of German rationalists ? Is it true that our Lord did not claim to be God, that He taught nothing definite, and gave no real authority to His Church to teach ? Of course these questions are far too big to be answered fully here. It would require several complete treatises. Here it is only possible to indicate the answers.

It is quite true that our Lord did not go about saying " I am God." That would have been entirely misunderstood, and would have so

E

shocked everyone by its suddenness that nobody would have listened to Him any further.
Moreover, that was not His way of teaching.
It was necessary to accustom His disciples
gradually to so novel an idea as that of God
made Man. He made the claim at first indirectly,
but He made it quite distinctly, and the evidence
for this is abundant in the first three Gospels.
He claimed powers which none but God could
properly claim. He amends the Law given by
God, He forgives sins, He requires that men shall
love Him more than father or mother or wife or
children, and be ready, if necessary, to leave them
all for His sake. He is greater than the Temple,
He is Lord of the Sabbath, He is greater than
Jonas, He alone is to be called Master, the angels
are His servants, and He will come again at the
end of the world to judge the living and the dead.
He habitually speaks of God the Father as " my
Father," " the Father " or " your Father," but
never as " our Father," clearly indicating that
He was not merely *a* son of God, as we all are,
but *the* Son of God in a quite unique sense.

Consequently, when He accepted from S Peter
the confession : " Thou art the Christ, the Son
of the living God," it is clear that the title was
both given and accepted in a sense quite different
from that of a mere human Messiah. He had

been deliberately trying to make His disciples understand that He was Divine. Therefore, when He approves Peter's confession and blesses him, it can only mean that He saw that Peter had really understood who He was, that He was none other than God the Son made Man.

But, still leaving out the Fourth Gospel, the supreme proof that He claimed to be God, and that His claim was so understood by His hearers, is that it was precisely for that that He was put to death. " The High Priest said to Him : I adjure thee, by the living God, that thou tell us if thou be the Christ the Son of God. Jesus saith to him : Thou hast said it. Nevertheless I say to you, hereafter you shall see the Son of Man sitting on the right hand of the power of God, and coming in the clouds of heaven. Then the High Priest rent his garments, saying : He hath blasphemed : what further need have we of witnesses ? Behold, now you have heard the blasphemy : What think you ? But they answering said : He is guilty of death." It is quite clear how the High Priest and the rest of the Sanhedrin understood His words. He was condemned for blasphemy, and merely to claim to be the Messiah was not blasphemy. They understood that He was claiming to be the Son of God in the sense of being Himself God. That was

blasphemy in their estimation. And He did not
retract or attempt to explain away His words.
For that claim He allowed Himself to be put to
death. There could not be a clearer acknowledgement that they had understood Him rightly.

But our authors say that He could not have
made this claim, because at first the Apostles
did not preach that He was God. Now, here
again it is true that they did not usually call
Him " God " straight out, because that would
certainly have been misunderstood. But they
did give Him titles which implied His Divinity,
and that from the very first. There is no gradual
development. That is simply a theory invented
by the rationalist critics to suit their ideas. In
Acts iii, 15, for example, He is called the Author
or Originator of Life (ἀρχηγός τῆς ζωῆς). But
most striking is the continual use of the title
Κύριος, Lord. " The Lord," " the Lord Jesus,"
" our Lord," " our Lord Jesus Christ " occur
constantly. Now, as everybody knows, this title,
when used in a religious sense, was applied by
the Jews to God only. It was the Septuagint
rendering of Adonai, which in reading the Old
Testament was substituted for the " unutterable
name " Jahweh. It is impossible to misunder-
stand the giving of this title to Jesus. It is used
indiscriminately of Him and of God the Father,

so that it is sometimes difficult to decide which is meant. In Acts x, 36, He is actually called " Lord of all." Who but God can be Lord of all ?

To speak of S Paul as " steadily working to this conclusion," namely, that our Lord is God, is an exceedingly strange way of describing his teaching. There is no working to a conclusion. His clear belief in our Lord's Divinity is there from the first. Not only are there the passages quoted by our authors, which in themselves plainly imply Divinity. And here it is necessary to point out that they give a very bad and misleading translation of Col. ii, 6. S Paul's words are οὐχ ἁρπαγμὸν ἡγήσατο τὸ εἶναι ἶσα θεῷ, and this they translate " thought it not an object of ambition to be made equal to God." In fact the old translation of the " Authorised Version " (which is also that of the Douai Version, and corresponds with the Vulgate), " thought it not robbery to be equal with God," seems to be clearly right. Lightfoot argues at great length that ἁρπαγμὸς ought to be translated "a prize, a treasure to be clutched at and retained at all hazards." His argument is not convincing, but at least it retains the sense that He *was* equal with God, which is what S Paul certainly means. There is no justification for rendering it " an object of ambition," and to translate τὸ εἶναι ἶσα

θεῷ " to be *made* equal to God " is monstrous.
To render the passage thus suggests that He was
not equal with God, and was quite content to
remain lower than God, since He " thought it
not an object of ambition to be made equal to
God," which is exactly the opposite of what
S Paul says. Whatever the exact meaning of
ἁρπαγμὸς there is no possible question of S Paul's
meaning that He *was* equal with God.

There are many other passages in S Paul
which are just as strong. For example, " All
things were created by Him and in Him, and by
Him all things consist." (Col. i, 17.) How could
that be said of anyone but God ? The Epistle
to the Hebrews also has many similar passages.
He " upholds all things by the word of His
power." (i, 3.) He is the One " for whom are
all things and by whom are all things." (ii, 10.)
In fact the Divinity of our Lord is quite plainly
taught throughout the New Testament. There
is no trace of a gradual development of the
idea. It was the clear conviction of all the
Apostles from the day of Pentecost onwards.

4. The next objection to the " oracular infallibility " is that the Church went wrong from the
very beginning. Not only did the Apostles not
teach our Lord's Divinity, but in what they did
teach they made grave mistakes. " If the teach-

ing of the Apostles was clear and definite about any single point, it was the imminence of the Second Coming of our Lord to judge both the quick and the dead." In that they were wrong. Consequently, they may have been equally wrong in anything else that they taught. We have no sort of guarantee that the Church did not go completely astray from the very first. That seems to be the argument, or at least the logical consequence of it.

But let us examine the facts which are supposed to prove the utter unreliability of the Apostles' teaching. Messrs. Milner-White and Knox must be well aware that a great deal has been written on this question of the Second Coming of our Lord, and that it cannot be settled off-hand by the quotation of a few texts. It is impossible here to go at length into the whole discussion. Those who wish to study the other side seriously should consult such works as those of Prat, Tillmann, Billot, Le Camus, Camerlynck and so forth. It will not do for Mr. Milner-White and Mr. Knox merely to set down a few texts, dogmatically assert that they prove their thesis, and brush aside every interpretation but their own as " special pleading."

In the first place, several of the passages quoted say nothing about the proximity or otherwise of our Lord's Coming. " Now it is high time for you to awake out of sleep, for now is our salvation nearer than when we believed. The night is far spent, the day is at hand." That may be said of us at any time, quite irrespective of the time of the Last Judgement. " We shall not all fall asleep, but we shall all be changed." That is true also. Although it suggests that the author expected to be one of those who would not fall asleep, it does not say so. Some of " us," that is, some Christians, will be alive at our Lord's Coming, whether it be to-morrow or a million years hence. " The day of the Lord cometh as a thief in the night." That says nothing about the time. It merely says that He will come suddenly, when people are least expecting it. In other passages the expressions are very vague. The word ἤγγικεν, for example, used in I Peter iv, 7, is very indefinite.

Again, what our authors say about S Paul's exhortation to the Thessalonians, in his Second Epistle to them, is singularly inaccurate. He distinctly tells them that the Coming is not so imminent as they suppose, because several things must happen first. (See II Thess. ii, 2 *seq.*)

And finally it has to be remembered that when the Sacred Writers speak of a future " coming " of the Lord it does not always necessarily refer to His last coming to judge all men. Our Lord comes in many other ways. He comes, for example, to each of us at death. He comes in many of the great crises of the world's history.

At the same time, comparing all the passages bearing on this matter, it does seem that there was a general expectation and hope among the Apostles, and the whole of the first generation of Christians, that the Last Coming would be very soon, and possibly, or even probably, in the lifetime of some of them. But this is clearly only their personal conjecture. It is not taught as an article of faith, or part of the Divine Revelation committed to them. On the contrary, they make it plain that they really know nothing about the time, for God has not revealed it.

That this was the case with S Paul is shown by the fact that his ideas on the subject changed as time went on. In his earlier Epistles (cf. I Thess. iv, 15, 16 ; I Cor. xv, 51) he seems to hope that the Lord will come in his lifetime. Already in II Corinthians he has begun to be less hopeful. (II Cor. v, 1–10.) In Philippians he looks for death as probable and desirable. (i, 19–26 ; ii, 17–23.) In II Timothy he has definitely concluded that his course is run and death is at hand. (II Tim. iv, 6 *seq*.) And this change in his attitude takes place without any sign that he is worried about it, or wonders why our Lord has not kept His promise ; which is very clear proof that he had no definite revelation on the matter. He knows that our Lord has not revealed the time of His coming. When he thought that it would probably be in his own lifetime it was merely a personal conjecture and hope.

All, therefore, that is " clear and definite " in the teaching of the Apostles on this matter is that our Lord *will* come again to judge the living and the dead, and that nobody knows the time. That is all that they teach as revealed by God, and in that they made no error.

The attempts, therefore, to prove that our Lord could not have meant what His words plainly mean is a total failure. The fact remains proved that He did found a Teaching Body, and gave to it authority and power to teach the Revelation of God without error to all generations until the end of the world. And Mr. Johnson's corollary to this, that the only Church which even claims to teach with such authority to-day is the " Roman " Church, is abundantly clear. That the Church of England does not do so is obvious. And certainly Messrs. Milner-White and Knox cannot maintain that it does, for they explicitly deny that any Church has, or ever had, the right to do so.

CHAPTER VI

S PETER IN THE NEW TESTAMENT

HAVING satisfied himself that our Lord founded His Church as a definite Teaching Body, to which He promised His abiding presence, so that it would always teach the truth revealed by Him with infallible authority, and that the " Roman " Church is the only Church to-day which even claims to speak with such authority, Mr. Johnson turned to the question of the Papacy.

By taking things in this order he shows that he saw the various questions connected with the claims of the Catholic Church in their right proportions. Many Anglicans talk as if the supremacy of the Pope were the primary question at issue between us and them. This is very far from being the case. The real question is whether our Lord founded a Teaching Body, to which He gave authority and power to teach infallibly the truth revealed by Him to all nations and all generations. One might almost say that that is the only question. For, if our Lord did form such a Body, and did make these promises to it, that Body must exist to-day. It must teach with authority, it must be world-wide, it must teach the same truth everywhere and always, and it must be one, undivided and indivisible.   I say that it must be one and indivisible, because a body that was split up into contending sections could not possibly teach in this authoritative way.   To say that the Church has been divided is to say that our Lord has failed to keep His promise, that He has failed to maintain in the world an authoritative Teaching Body, as He promised to do.

Now, the only body in the world to-day which corresponds with this description is that which our Anglican friends call the " Roman " Church, that is the Catholic Church.   Therefore the Catholic Church is the Church founded by Christ, the Church to which He made the promise of infallible guidance.   Therefore whatever the Catholic Church teaches we can confidently accept. But among other things the Catholic Church teaches that the Pope is its supreme and infallible Head on earth, the successor of S Peter, whom our Lord appointed to be its first Head.   Therefore this must be true.   I can accept the Papacy on the authority of the Catholic Church, and have no need to make researches into its history.

However, it certainly strengthens our position if we can show that there is abundant independent evidence for the fact that our Lord did appoint

S Peter to be Head of the Church, and that the Popes are his successors. Therefore Mr. Johnson was quite right to examine the evidence, and in fact he sets it out in his book very clearly and well.

But we have to examine the objections raised by Mr. Milner-White and Mr. Knox. They begin by making fun of Mr. Johnson for having counted the number of times that S Peter's name is mentioned in the Gospels and Acts, compared with those of the other Apostles, as if he had rested his whole argument on that. In fact it is mentioned merely as the first fact that struck him. He goes on through twenty-five pages to show in detail what the position of S Peter in the Gospels and Acts really is, and to draw out the meaning of our Lord's promises to him. But to all this Messrs. Milner-White and Knox have hardly a word to answer.

Only two other passages in all these twenty-five pages are criticised. The first is that in which Mr. Johnson points out, quite correctly, that " the titles conferred on S Peter by our Lord, such as Foundation Stone, Keybearer and Shepherd, were titles known by all the Apostles as Messianic and as belonging to our Lord Himself." This, they say, implies that the Pope is " a perpetual re-incarnation " ; " it is the plain implication of his words " ! Is this really to be

taken seriously ? To any ordinary mind they
do not even hint at such an absurdity. They
merely mean that, as the Pope is our Lord's
Representative on earth, His Messianic titles
can be applied in a secondary sense to him.
Several functions which are primarily those of
our Lord Himself are carried out by the Pope as
His Vicar. Our Lord is the real Foundation
Stone on which the Church rests, but in a
secondary sense, and in complete dependence on
Him, the Pope is. And so with the other titles.

The other passage which is criticised is the
reference to the famous occasion when S Paul
" withstood Peter to the face." Here we are
told that S Paul " corrected [Peter] on the vital
question of faith and morals." This is an old
Protestant argument that has been answered
many times. There was in fact no question of
faith and morals. The principle of the equality
of Jew and Gentile had been settled by S Peter
himself, and accepted by the Council in Jerusalem
described in Acts xv. It was merely a question
of whether it might not be wise on some occa-
sions to yield to Jewish prejudices by refraining
from eating with Gentile Christians. (There is
no mention of the Eucharist.) S Peter himself
generally did eat with Gentile Christians, but
he thought that on this occasion it would be

continue always. Our Lord told the Apostles to baptise, but He did not say explicitly that their successors, if they had any, were to go on baptising. In fact, if we argue in this way, we can do anything we like with the Church of God. There would be no reason to suppose that any of our Lord's arrangements were to be permanent. But of course that is absurd. The constitution of the Church must remain as our Lord settled it.

Again, the very titles that our Lord used in describing the office of Peter imply permanence. Peter was to be the Rock, the solid foundation, on which the Church was to stand firm for ever. Could any term more distinctly imply permanence? If the Primacy was to be a merely temporary thing He should have described Peter as a scaffolding. A scaffolding is taken away when the building is complete, but it is not usual to cut away the foundation as soon as you have got the roof on.

It is quite true that our Lord did not mention Rome as the future seat of the Primacy. But if the Bishop of Rome is not the successor of S Peter, who is? There is no other claimant, and never has been. From the second century at least the Bishops of Rome have claimed to be the successors of Peter, and to have a Primacy over the whole Church. Nobody else has ever made such a claim, and for many centuries nobody thought of denying it. The Popes were often resisted, but their position was not disputed. It is remarkable how all the early heretics even tried to get the approval of the Pope, although in fact they never succeeded.

Our authors' next objection is a curious one. They tell us that there is a " quite serious doubt whether S Peter ever went to Rome at all." This rather reminds me of the people who have tried to prove that Jesus of Nazareth never existed. There have been quite a number of them : Bruno Bauer, Loman, Edwin Johnson, Emile Burnouff, Vollers, Arthur Drews, and several more. Of course it is possible to make out a case denying any historical fact.

I do not know whether it is worth while going into this question. The facts are quite clear that our Lord made S Peter Head of His Church, that this Headship was to be a permanent office, and that the Bishops of Rome are his successors in that office. Therefore, if the existing evidence for S Peter's residence were scanty it would not make very much difference. The Pope's claims are not founded on what historical evidence happens to have remained for the fact of S Peter's residence in Rome. They rest on a much broader basis than that, and we should not be disturbed if there were no evidence at all for his having gone to Rome. But in fact the evidence is abundant. It is so abundant that very few, even of the most irresponsible Protestant assailants of the Papacy, have ventured to dispute it.

Of course nobody attaches any importance to the Pseudo-Clementine writings. We can only suppose that they are dragged in in order to create the impression that the evidence is all unreliable. But in fact no respectable writer would think of using them as evidence. Apart, however, from the Pseudo-Clement, Mr. Milner-White and Mr. Knox tell us that practically the only evidence is that of Hegesippus, who visited Rome about A.D. 165. They say that " he seems to have found no list of Bishops of Rome, and to have compiled one as best he could." And then we are told (without any attempt at proof) that Irenaeus copied Hegesippus, and all later writers copied either Irenaeus or the Pseudo-Clementine legend.

Now, to begin with, when Hegesippus visited Rome in A.D. 165, he may or may not have found a list of the Bishops of Rome, but he certainly was told by the Roman Christians that their first Bishop was S Peter, and surely they ought to have known, even if a century had elapsed. A century is not such a very long time. There must have been many people living in Rome in

A.D. 165 whose fathers would have told them about S Peter's being there. People who talk about a century being such a long time that it gives room for all kinds of legends to arise do not use their imagination. To take a parallel from our own times, how many people there must be alive to-day whose fathers have told them all about the passing of the Reform Bill in 1832. So in 165 there must have been many people whose fathers had told them all about S Peter having been there, and handing on the Primacy to Linus. It is perfectly gratuitous to say that the Romans at that date ascribed the foundation of their Church to Peter and Paul because, having read the Acts, those were the only two Apostles they knew anything about. At that date they must have been perfectly aware of the facts.

Again, it is a mere assumption and extremely unlikely that Irenaeus merely copied Hegesippus. Irenaeus had been to Rome himself and had made independent enquiries. And it is an equally baseless and unlikely assumption that all later writers copied Irenaeus or the Pseudo-Clementine writings. By the middle of the third century it was the tradition accepted all over the world, by Cyprian in Carthage, by Firmilian in Cæsarea, by Dionysius in Alexandria, by Fabius in Antioch, that the Bishop of Rome was the successor of S Peter. What evidence is there that all this came from Hegesippus? It is exceedingly unlikely that so universal a tradition arose out of one man having been told a baseless legend in Rome.

But in fact there is direct evidence that the tradition did not all come from that one source. The words of S Ignatius are not explicit, but they certainly seem to imply that Peter and Paul were the Apostles of Rome who " gave them orders." And Clement's allusion to them does not seem to have much meaning unless he intends to include them among the martyrs of Rome. But these are not the only other witnesses by any means. Eusebius tells us plainly of three other authorities of the second century—the Roman presbyter Caius, Dionysius of Corinth and Papias. Furthermore, there is the testimony of an anonymous writing of the second century called *Pauli Prædicatio*, and the Muratorian Fragment mentions S Peter's martyrdom at Rome.

Then we are told that " the allusions to them scribbled on the walls prove nothing more than that about A.D. 140 the names of the Apostles were familiar to Roman Christians." In case some readers may not know the facts, it may be well to mention that under the Church of San Sebastiano there was discovered some years ago

a wall covered, not with " allusions," but with
invocations to S Peter and S Paul, in the very
spot where, according to tradition, the bodies of
the Apostles temporarily rested. To most
people this seems very strong confirmation of
the tradition. Why should multitudes of pil-
grims have visited that particular spot, and
written these invocations just there, unless that
spot had had some special connection with the
two Apostles ?

The argument that the " Church in Babylon "
cannot mean Rome is very weak. The fact that
S Peter exhorts Christians to submit themselves
to the King and other civil governors for God's
sake, " as unto them that are sent by Him for
the punishment of evildoers and the praise of
them that do well," does not preclude him from
knowing that Rome was a sink of iniquity,
parallel to the Babylon of old. There is no
contradiction at all. Are we to suppose that,
because S Paul gives a similar command to
" honour the king," he must have regarded Nero
as a model of virtue ? In any case it is hardly
conceivable that S Peter wrote from the actual
Babylon, since Josephus tells us that the Jewish
community there was practically destroyed.

The argument that the Roman Church was one
of the last to accept the First Epistle of S Peter

as genuine is equally poor, for if it was written from there, that is precisely the place where they would not have a copy. The copies would be in the places to which they were sent: Pontus, Galatia, Cappadocia, Asia and Bithynia.[1]

At the end of this chapter there is a curious Note III. It has nothing to do with Mr. Johnson's book, and it is not easy to see why it is there. But as a sample of our authors' methods it is most interesting. The method is to set down the most doubtful theories of rationalistic critics as incontrovertible facts, and then label any statements contrary to those theories as "methods of propaganda current in the Roman Catholic underworld."

Thus we are told off-hand that the well-known passage in S Ignatius, where he addresses the Roman Church as "the Church which presides in the place of the region of the Romans," is "a mere recognition of the headship of the Roman Church in Italy." Why Italy? The "place of the region of the Romans" is Rome. It is there that she presides, but over what? The first question is why S Ignatius uses the word "presides" at all. He addresses other Churches simply as "the Church which is in Tralles," or

[1] For further criticism of this strange theory see the fifth essay in *Religions of Authority and the Religion of the Spirit*, by Abbot Butler. (Sheed and Ward).

" the Church which is in Ephesus," and so forth.
Rome has a different position from other
Churches ; she " presides " over something. Over
what ? There is no mention of Italy. The statement is quite general that she presides. Further
on she is described as " presiding over the love."
This is a very curious phrase, but the most
probable interpretation seems to be " presiding
over the union of Christians." The question is
discussed at length by Dom John Chapman in
the Revue Bénédictine, 1896, and that is his
opinion. Messrs. Milner-White and Knox may
think that he has not proved it to be true, but
they should not dismiss the reasoned opinions of
such a scholar without any attempt to disprove
them as " methods of propaganda current in the
Roman Catholic underworld." That is not the
kind of treatment which scholars of any opinions
are accustomed to receive in Cambridge.

But their statements about the Epistle of
Clement are simply amazing. We are calmly
informed that " there is *no evidence*[1] that the
writer's name was Clement." Now, if they had
tried to argue that the evidence is insufficient,
it would have been intelligible. But to say that
there is *none* is manifestly untrue. I need not
go into the evidence in detail here, for it can be

---

[1] The italics are mine.

found clearly set out in Lightfoot's edition of S Clement—evidence so strong that Lightfoot justly says that " there can be no reasonable doubt about the authorship." I am aware that since then some critics of the newer school, who are prepared to cast doubts on everything, have tried to explain that evidence away. Nevertheless it remains.

Then we are told that if the author's name was Clement, " there is *no real reason*[1] for supposing that it was Pope Clement." Here again I must be content to refer to Lightfoot.

But finally it is asserted that " there is the very gravest reason to doubt whether any such person as Clement was Bishop of Rome at all." This grave reason, however, is merely the fact that the author of the Simon Magus legends, which everybody admits to be fiction, has omitted his two predecessors. That is supposed to throw grave doubts on the existence of Clement. By similar reasoning, if we were to find an old romance, in which King Stephen was made the immediate successor of William the Conqueror, it would throw grave doubt on the existence of William, and look as if he were a legendary figure who " had to be fitted in somewhere." And then they complain of " the methods of propaganda of the Roman Catholic underworld " !

[1] The italics are mine.

CHAPTER VII

THE PAPACY IN HISTORY

THIS chapter begins by suggesting " a possible reply " to the argument of the preceding chapter : " It might be urged that although it is possible for historians to throw doubt on the connection of Peter with Rome, yet the necessity of the Papacy in the Church proves that the foundation on which it rests its claims is a guarantee that it must be right." And on this imagined reply they comment thus : " It is a perilous argument. First you claim that history supports the claims of the Papacy ; and when history is undecided you claim that the Papacy proves the truth of the facts which history regards as doubtful."

No doubt this is a *possible* reply, in the sense that it is possible that a lunatic might argue in that way. But why deal with the possible replies of lunatics rather than with those that we actually make ? We do not admit for a moment that " history is undecided." The evidence is perfectly clear that our Lord made S Peter the first Head of His Church on earth, that He intended the Headship to be permanent, and that it has continued to the present day in the line of Popes.

For further confirmation of the correctness of our interpretation of our Lord's commission to S Peter we do certainly use other arguments. We do not speak of the *necessity* of the Papacy, for it is conceivable that our Lord might have founded a different kind of Church without an earthly Head. We can only point to the eminent suitability of the Church having an earthly Head. We may say that it is very difficult to imagine how the necessary unity of the Church could have been provided for otherwise. And we certainly do point to the marvellous way in which the Papacy has fulfilled its function of preserving the unity of the Church, and of keeping it faithful to the truth revealed by Christ, guiding it through the shoals and rocks and quicksands of heresy, as an additional argument that it is of Divine origin.

We also point to the disasters that have overtaken those bodies of Christians who have broken away from the Rock on which the Church of Christ stands firm. On the one hand there are the Eastern Churches. Some of them have fallen into manifest heresy, and although the group of Churches known as " Orthodox " have in the main kept the Faith (excepting their heresy in the matter of the *Filioque*, and in their denial of the Papal Supremacy), it has been at the cost of becoming fossilised and sterile. They have ceased to think, and merely repeat in parrot fashion the decisions of the first seven General Councils. And then there are the Protestant Churches, where there is nothing but chaos.

Messrs. Milner-White and Knox, however, in this chapter on " The Papacy in History," do not deal with these matters. They merely attack once more the dogma of Papal Infallibility, and against this they appear to have three arguments.

1. The first is certainly original. They argue that the Vatican Council does not really say that the Pope is infallible, for it only says that he has " that infallibility with which the Divine Redeemer willed that His Church should be endowed." But, " if you choose not to believe that our Lord willed that His Church should be endowed with any infallibility whatsoever, then you can accept the definition. You believe that the Pope is endowed with the infallibility which our Lord conferred on His Church because He did not endow His Church with any infallibility at all."

Yes, certainly, and if you further choose to say that our Lord was not God, you need not pay any attention to what He willed. The Vatican Council was defining the Faith on a point on which doubts had been raised. The infallibility of the Church was accepted by all Catholics, and is here presupposed. But I do not think that many of the readers of " One God and Father of All " will pay much attention to a quibble of this kind.

2. The next argument is a little more plausible. It amounts to this. It is not always possible to be certain whether a particular papal decision is an infallible utterance or not. Indeed our authors go so far as to say that there are only two, of which we can be quite certain, and we are only sure that they were uttered *ex cathedra*, " because the great majority of Roman Catholic theologians think that they were." And so they go on : " What is the good of an Infallible Authority if you hardly ever use it, and don't even know that you have used it until everyone has agreed with it ? . . . It would seem that we need yet another Infallible Authority to say whether the Infallible Authority has spoken infallibly, and then perhaps another Infallible Authority to say whether the second Infallible Authority was speaking infallibly when it said that the first Infallible Authority was speaking infallibly, and so *ad infinitum*." And so they

seem to imply that those deluded Protestants,
who are " worried with modern difficulties," and
to whom " an Infallible Authority sounds attrac-
tive," and who, therefore, " go over to Rome,"
find no more certainty in the Catholic Church
than they did in the Church of England, but
discover that the so-called Infallible Authority
is a snare and a delusion.

All this sounds plausible. The falsity of it is
proved by the simple fact that on all really vital
questions we *have* got certainty. If you read any
Catholic text-book of theology, you will find a
very large number of doctrines stated as being
de fide, and you will find precisely the same
doctrines set down as *de fide* in every other
text-book. Furthermore, if any misguided priest
were to teach doctrines contrary to these, he
would promptly find himself called over the coals
by his bishop, whoever that bishop might be.
And if by some strange aberration a bishop
taught anything contrary to them, he would be
promptly summoned to Rome to give an account
of himself. And in either case, if the delinquent
persisted in his wrong teaching he would, if a
priest, be deprived of his faculties, or if a bishop,
deprived of his see. And if the persistence
continued, this would be followed by
excommunication.

You have only to compare this with the notorious state of affairs in the Church of England, where there is no agreement even about the most fundamental doctrines. One clergyman teaches that in the Communion Service the bread and wine are really changed into the Body and Blood of Christ, while another says that that is a gross superstition, and that they simply remain bread and wine. One teaches that the Sacrament of Penance is normally necessary for the forgiveness of mortal sin after Baptism, while the other says that there is no such thing as a Sacrament of Penance, and that nobody has any real power to absolve sinners, except in the sense of making a general statement that if the sinner is truly penitent he is forgiven. Of course they all appeal to the words of the Book of Common Prayer and so forth to support their views, but there is nobody to decide which is right.

If I may here venture again on a personal note, it was precisely this intolerable uncertainty which made it impossible for me to continue in the ministry of the Church of England. I had been accustomed to teach what I thought to be true, and to be in accordance with the authorised formularies of the Church of England. But the clergyman in the neighbouring parish taught something quite different, while a third clergyman in the parish on the other side taught things different from either of us, and there was nobody to decide which was right. It became clear to me that I was simply teaching my own opinions, and I realised what impertinence that was. Why should I expect people to receive my opinions rather than those of other clergymen who differed from me in various directions? *Now* I do not teach my opinions, but what I know to be the teaching of the Church. I have no doubt at all what the teaching of the Church is; it is the same as is taught by every other Catholic priest throughout the world, and if any of us were to make a mistake we should very quickly be put right.

Now, what makes this difference? How does it come about that we in the Catholic Church are all agreed, and that any mistake is speedily corrected, if there is no means of finding out for certain what the Church really teaches? It is open to anyone to argue that the Authority is wrong, and that its claim to be infallible is a monstrous imposture. But what is quite clear about it is that it does know its own mind, and that it is quite easy to be certain of its mind on any point in the large body of doctrine that is called *de fide*.

Where, then, is the flaw in our authors' argument ? In the first place they make the mistake of isolating the infallibility of the Pope from that of the Church. It is primarily the Church that is infallible, and that is the fact that matters most. It is that in this definite Teaching Body, which is the Roman Catholic Church, we have an infallible teacher, which is able to hand down the truth revealed by God, and explain it as need arises without error. The question of the infallibility of the Pope is a question of the organ through which the mind of the Church is expressed. Infallible definitions are given either by a General Council ratified by the Pope, or by the Pope alone, having explored the mind of the Church in some other way.

In fact Popes have made infallible decisions without a General Council much more often than twice. A few obvious examples are to be found in the Bull of Boniface VIII *Unam Sanctam*, the Constitution *Benedictus Deus* of Benedict XII, the *Exsurge Domine* of Leo X against the heresies of Luther, and the *Cum Occasione* of Innocent X against the Jansenists, all of which manifestly contain *ex cathedra* decisions. But if in most cases definitions have been made by means of General Councils it makes no difference. The important thing is that we *have* an infallible

G

teacher that is capable of making its voice heard.

Again, it must be borne in mind that, even when the Pope is acting in conjunction with a General Council, either presiding at it or confirming its decrees, he is still using his infallible teaching power, for it is only when the decrees of Councils have been ratified or in some way accepted by the Pope, that we can be sure that they are infallible decisions. If the Popes had never done more than that they would have made a very ample use of their power, and the importance of having a Pope would have been manifest. For there have been other councils claiming to be General Councils besides the twenty which are accepted as such. But how do we know which are genuine and which are not ? Only those are genuinely General in which the Pope has taken part as Head of the Church, using his infallible authority to confirm their decrees.

And finally it is not true that we only know that definitions are infallible " because the great majority of Roman Catholic theologians think they are." We know they are when it is made clear by the Pope's own words that he intended to " define a doctrine concerning faith or morals to be held by the whole Church." Consider, for example, the words in which Pius IX defined the

Immaculate Conception : " By the authority of our Lord Jesus Christ, of the Blessed Apostles Peter and Paul and Our own we declare, pronounce and define that the doctrine which holds that the Blessed Virgin Mary in the first moment of her conception was by a singular grace and privilege of Almighty God, through the foreseen merits of Jesus Christ the Saviour of the human race, preserved from all stain of original sin, has been revealed by God and is therefore to be firmly and constantly believed by all the Faithful. Wherefore, if any presume to think in their hearts otherwise than has been defined by Us (which may God avert), let them know and understand that they are condemned by their own judgement, that they have made shipwreck concerning the Faith and fallen away from the unity of the Church." It needs no opinion of a majority of theologians to tell us what the Pope intended to do here.

Messrs. Milner-White and Knox complain that " to Anglo-Catholics worried with modern difficulties " the Infallible Authority of the Pope is useless " for the simple reason that it has never dealt with them." I do not quite know to what kind of difficulties they refer. Probably they refer to difficulties raised against the Faith by Biblical critics, or historians or scientists. But

it is not the business of the Authority to answer
these difficulties. Its function is to *define* the
Faith, not to argue about it, or to defend it, or
to show how objections can be answered. These
are matters for theologians and scholars, and
there are plenty such in the Catholic Church
who are doing their work exceedingly well,
although Messrs. Milner-White and Knox do
not seem to be aware of their existence.

It is not, however, the failure to find an answer
to these questions in the Church of England or
the hope of doing so in the Catholic Church,
that leads a good number of " Anglo-Catholics "
and others every year to " Rome." It is the
failure of the Church of England to teach anything definite on the most fundamental doctrines
of the Faith, and the knowledge that " Rome "
does. The Catholic Church does not profess to
have a solution ready for every critical, historical
or scientific problem, but it does profess to
teach, and it does teach, those supernatural
truths revealed by God, which concern our
eternal salvation. That is what the Catholic
Church does, and what the Church of England
does not do. It is the failure to do that which
made many of us leave the Church of England,
and it is the Catholic Church's success in doing
it which makes us find peace and security there.

The statement that the Papacy " begins by making far-reaching claims and gradually reduces them because it has been proved to have used them badly " is a mere travesty of history. The fact is that from the beginning everybody believed the Church to be the infallible teacher, and they believed that in the Church the Pope was the supreme teacher, who must therefore have some kind of infallibility. Until it was defined it was rather vague. Some people, no doubt, thought it had a wider extension than it really has. Others, on the contrary, were inclined to minimise it, and the Gallicans denied it altogether. Now that it has been defined we know more precisely what it really means.

The action of Pius V towards Elizabeth is given as an example of a Papal claim that has now been abandoned. What Pius V did was to declare that Elizabeth had so violated the rights of her subjects that they were released from all duties of loyalty to her. I am not aware that the Holy See has ever abandoned the claim to make such a pronouncement in future if the circumstances should require it. And in any case what has this got to do with infallibility ? Did Pius V on that occasion define a doctrine concerning faith or morals to be held by the whole Church ?

3. Our authors' third argument against the infallibility of the Pope is indeed a curious one. Our old friends Liberius, Honorius and the Galileo case have apparently been abandoned, no doubt because those objections have been so often and so conclusively answered. Instead of these we have a new objection. It has not even the plausibility of the older ones, but on the other hand it has the advantage of so appealing to not very logical people as to stir up their prejudices against the Catholic Church.

Briefly, the argument is that the Papacy has in the past approved of the " persecution " of heretics. But this enlightened age knows that complete toleration of every kind of teaching in the matter of religion is the only right course. Therefore in approving of " persecution " the Papacy made a grievous mistake. Therefore it cannot be infallible.

Here we may notice in the first place that our authors flatly contradict the whole argument of the first part of this chapter. There they argued that the claim to infallibility was so limited that the infallible authority had hardly ever, and perhaps never, been exercised. Now it is made to include every action of which any Popes in the past have in any way approved. Either argument by itself might be plausible, but they really cannot have it both ways.

To talk about the wickedness of the Inquisition is an unfailing way of stirring up animosity against the Catholic Church in the minds of those who have not studied the history of the time in which the Inquisition was instituted. It was in fact instituted by Lucius III in 1184 to help in the repression of the neo-Manichæan sects, Catharists and so forth, which were the plague of Europe at the time. It was not the Church which began to repress these heretics by force, but the civil powers, warmly supported by popular opinion. The policy was begun by Robert, King of France, in 1017, and his example was soon followed by others. The reason of their action was simply that those heretics taught doctrines which threatened to overthrow the whole established social order. They had to be suppressed, because they were the enemies of society.

Even so, however, it was a long time before the Church could be persuaded to have anything to do with the use of force. We find Pope after Pope counselling moderation, and saying that these heretics ought to be converted by exhortations and reasoning rather than suppressed by force. It was only when these methods proved to be wholly inadequate, and the heresies grew to such an extent as to threaten the destruction of the whole social order, that the Church was obliged to admit that the time had come when the use of force was necessary. And, since that was the case, it was obviously desirable that the civil and ecclesiastical authorities should work in concert. It belongs to the ecclesiastical authorities to judge what is heresy, and who are heretics, and to the civil authorities to punish those who have been thus convicted.

There was no change of principle. The Church's principle was that milder methods must be tried first, but that when they have manifestly failed, then certainly subverters of the social order must be repressed by force, whether they are ordinary thieves and murderers, or anarchists, or such heretics as the Catharists. Anyone who denies that principle must advocate the abolition of all punishment of crime.

Nobody denies that in the course of the Inquisition excesses were committed, especially in Spain. But that was the fault of individuals, and the continual action of the Popes was to endeavour to prevent such excesses, exhorting the local authorities to moderation and often revoking their sentences. There is a whole series of such actions by Gregory IX, Innocent IV, Honorius IV, Boniface VIII and Clement V.

But Messrs. Milner-White and Knox maintain that in any case these arguments could not apply to the " beliefs of the Reformation," which were " socially harmless." I reply by simply denying that the beliefs of the Reformation were socially harmless. The Reformation produced the most disastrous social results, of which we have not yet seen the end. European civilisation was built upon the foundation of the Catholic Faith and Catholic order. The Reformation struck at the roots of that order. It destroyed the unity of Europe, it immediately produced a lowering of the moral standard, and it was the beginning of that disintegration of Christianity of which we see the results to-day. For Protestantism is a disintegrating force. It leads inevitably in the long run to rationalism, to contempt of all authority, human and Divine, to unrestrained competition, to the accumulation of wealth in the hands of a few, and finally to such reactions as Socialism, Communism and Bolshevism. Those who wish to see all this proved at length should study " An Essay on the Economic Effects of the Reformation," by George O'Brien. They will then be able to judge for themselves whether the doctrines of the Reformation were " socially harmless."

This chapter has again a very curious note at

the end. " The uselessness," we are told, " of
an infallible Church in this matter is shown by
the fact that it did nothing considerable in the
suppression of slavery in the nineteenth century.
The suppression of slavery, and of suttee in India,
were due to the influence on the governments
concerned of the Evangelical bodies."

What this has got to do with infallibility is not
clear, but the argument in itself is amusing. The
Catholic Church is shown to be " useless " in
this matter, because it was not the Catholic
Church but Evangelicals like Wilberforce and
Clarkson who finally induced the British Government to take the initiative in the suppression
of the modern slave trade. All honour to
Wilberforce, Clarkson and the rest, that they at
last persuaded the British Government to this
tardy act of reparation. But is it really the
fault of the Catholic Church that the British
Government had failed to take such steps before ?
Was the British Government in the sixteenth,
seventeenth and eighteenth centuries so favour-
able to the Catholic Church that a word from the
Pope would have stirred it to instant action ?
The Popes, in fact, never ceased to denounce
slavery ever since its revival in the New World
at the end of the fifteenth century. Unfortunately
Europe would not listen. So that our authors'

argument may be put in a sentence : An infallible teaching Church is shown to be useless,
because people who refuse to listen to it and
deny its authority are not much influenced by it !

CHAPTER VIII

AUTHORITY IN RELIGION

" **B**UT," our authors imagine an objector saying, " it is no use for you to level all these destructive criticisms at the Roman view of authority unless you have some alternative to offer. What is your guarantee against a general relapse of mankind into religious and moral chaos if you have not a living voice to speak with authority in the confusion of the present age ? " And on this very pertinent objection they make the following curious comment : " The difficulty seems to show a peculiar lack of trust in the power of God to guide His Church."

The difficulty shows no lack of trust in the power of God to guide His Church. We entirely trust God to guide His Church in the way that He promised. He founded the Church to teach the truth revealed by Him to all nations and all generations, and we trust Him so to guide it that it will always do so without error. If the Church had no living voice to speak with authority it would mean that God had ceased to guide it

But let us continue. As a proof that there is no need for a living voice to speak with authority we are told that God guided His Church through the first two centuries, and enabled it to overcome the Gnostic heresies " without finding it necessary to use the infallible voice." These heresies were " met by the Church and eliminated without either a Pope or a General Council. The Bishops of Rome were silent ; it would have been impossible for Councils to meet in an age of persecution ; and the Church carried on without the voice of either."

This is a very strange statement. I should have said that there never was a time when the infallible voice of the Church was clearer, and that it was precisely that infallible voice and nothing else which " eliminated " the Gnostic heresies. Gnosticism was " eliminated " by being rejected by the Bishops of all the principal sees of Christendom, as contrary to the Apostolic tradition. There was no occasion for the Popes to make any pronouncement on the matter *urbi et orbi*, and still less to summon a General Council, even if it had been possible, for all the Bishops of the principal sees stood firm in their opposition. But the Bishop of Rome was by no means " silent." It is well known that most of the Gnostic leaders made desperate efforts to

obtain recognition at Rome. Valentinus did,
and Cerdo, and Marcion and many others. As
the distinguished Protestant scholar Caspari puts
it, they were particularly anxious to gain recognition in Rome "in order thereby to get easier
access elsewhere, and to be enabled to spread with
more force. The dignity of the Church of Rome
was to cover them in their efforts ; she was, so
to speak, to stamp them with the hall-mark of
Christianity and Catholicity or orthodoxy."
When, therefore, these heretics were decisively rejected, as they all were, by successive Popes, it
is clear that those Popes were taking a very
leading part in the "elimination" of Gnosticism.

Moreover, it was precisely to the living voice
of the Church, and more particularly to that of
the Church of Rome, that S Irenaeus appealed
in his efforts to deal with the Gnostics. His argument was that their doctrines were contrary to
that of the Apostolic Churches, and especially to
that of Rome. According to him the living voice
of the Church of Rome is in itself quite sufficient
to refute all the heretics. The passage is well
known : "But since it would be very long in a
volume of this sort to give the succession of all
the Churches, we will point to that of the exceedingly great and ancient Church which was
founded and established at Rome by the most

glorious Apostles Peter and Paul. By its tradition and by its ' faith announced to men,' which has been transmitted to us by the successions of Bishops, we confound all those who in any way, by caprice or vainglory, or by blindness and perversity of will, gather where they ought not. . . . The Blessed Apostles, therefore, having founded and built the Church, entrusted to Linus the office of Bishop." There follows a list of the Bishops down to Eleutherius, and then he continues : " In the same order and in the same teaching the tradition of the Church from the Apostles and the preaching of the truth has come down to us. And this is a most complete proof that it is one and the same life-giving Faith which has been preserved in the Church from the Apostles until now, and handed down in truth."

The living voice of the Church, then, at that time was perfectly clear, and nothing further was needed to make it clear than the ordinary teaching of the Bishops of Rome and the other Apostolic Churches, which were all agreed. But later on came a terrible time, when there was disagreement among the Bishops themselves on the most fundamental doctrines, such as that of our Lord's Divinity. Then other means had to be adopted to make it clear what the true voice of the Church was.

In the opinion of Messrs. Milner-White and Knox the Bishops of the Catholic Church to-day are not only those in communion with Rome, but all the "Orthodox," and all the Anglican Bishops as well, including Bishop Barnes. Now, if these Bishops were all as completely agreed on every matter as the primitive Bishops were in their opposition to Gnosticism, we might be content to accept their unanimous teaching as the living voice of the Church. But since that is not the case we have to look elsewhere for the organ of that voice.

Our authors now proceed to explain their own idea of Authority. They begin with one of their customary sneers at Mr. Johnson's lack of scholarship. "It is one of the most pathetic features," they write, "of 'One Lord, One Faith,' that the author simply collects all the references to authority in the English Authorised Version and assumes that the word 'authority' means the same thing in each case. It is an assumption which any competent scholar would have told him was quite unfounded." And then they explain that what they understand by authority is "that which gives us reason for believing." It is quite possible that Mr. Johnson did not go further than the Authorised Version. I do not know. But if he had, would it have made so much difference ? In all the passages to which he refers, with one exception, the word 'authority' is used in the Authorised Version to translate the Greek word ἐξουσία. The exception is Tit. ii, 15, where the word is ἐπιταγή, which means very much the same as ἐξουσία. One or two other words with rather different meanings are translated " authority " in other passages, but they have nothing to do with our present subject.

What does the word ἐξουσία mean ? It means primarily the right and power to do something, and then it is also used to designate a person or body of persons endowed with such right and power. And this is also the proper meaning of the English word authority. Messrs. Milner-White and Knox want the word authority to mean " that which gives us reason for believing." But this is *not* the meaning of the word, and to use it in that sense is to confuse the issue and to make any intelligible discussion impossible. Authority means the right and power to do something, as any dictionary would tell them. And the question about Authority is this. Believing, as we do, that God has given a Revelation to mankind, we want to know who has the right and the power to teach that Revelation, and whether it is a power to teach it infallibly, and if not, what exactly it is.

H

Since Messrs. Milner-White and Knox reject our answers to these questions, we should have expected them to give an alternative answer of their own. They do arrive at some kind of answer later on, and that we must consider when we come to it. But in the meantime we must follow the discussion of " authority " in their own peculiar meaning of the term, as " that which gives us reason for believing." And we are told that there are two and only two such " authorities." One is " the Person of our Lord," and the other is " the private judgement of the individual."

" What finally causes men and women to believe in the Christian Faith," they say, " is the fact that they find in [our Lord] something which claims at once their love, obedience and worship." No doubt that must be the starting point, and it must always remain the centre of all true religion. But to have found something in our Lord which claims love, obedience and worship does not in itself cause you to believe in anything that can reasonably be called " the Christian Faith." That expression implies a definite body of truth, and you have not discovered that by the mere fact of being attracted to our Lord's Person, and being moved to love, obey and worship Him. Before you can believe

" the Christian Faith," you must know what it is, and have some assurance that it is true. Mere love for our Lord's Person will not at once give you that.

So we proceed to our second " authority," which is " the private judgement of the individual." " Men are drawn to Christianity," they say, " by the Person of our Lord, but only because their own private judgement accepts Him as supplying what they need. And it is their own private judgement that assents to the dogmatic system, which explains to them why the particular religious society, which they desire to join, claims to be the truth, or to possess a larger measure of truth than other societies with somewhat different systems."

They then proceed at great length to show that the acceptance of any one of the various systems claiming to be the Christian Faith must be an act of private judgement, and that " even if your private judgement comes to the conclusion that it is a good thing to submit your private judgement to the claims of Rome, it is still an act of your own private judgement that submits." They apologise " if [they] seem to have given too much space to a rather obvious point," but " it is a point which Roman controversialists do their best to confuse." It is indeed a very obvious

point, but I have not found " Roman controversialists " doing their best to confuse it. Of course
it is by an act of private judgement (assisted by
the grace of God) that anyone accepts the claims
of the Catholic Church. But then our authors
go on to say that it is " ridiculous " to suppose
that any ordinary person can trust his own judgement when he decides that the Catholic Church
is a reliable teacher, but cannot trust it to the
extent of settling every disputed theological
question by himself. Why is it ridiculous ? It
seems to me to be plain common sense.

Consider the position. I have somehow been
attracted to the Personality of our Lord, and
have seen that He is worthy of " love, obedience
and worship." But in order to obey Him I
must find out what He taught. According to
Messrs. Milner-White and Knox there is no way
of doing so but the use of my own private judgement. Very well, I set about the task. I find
several hundreds of Christian sects, teaching
different doctrines on every conceivable point.
In some sects, like the Church of England, I find
almost as great divergence between one minister
and another. And then I suppose I must take
account also of the theories of such people as
Harnack and Schweitzer, who have their own
remarkable ideas as to what our Lord taught.

But there is no help for it, I must puzzle out each one of the hundred questions on which they differ, and decide each one separately for myself and answer it by my own private judgement.

Bewildered by this gigantic task I look round and find one, and by far the greatest, of the Christian communities, which says : " Of course you cannot work out all these questions for yourself with any assurance that you will decide them rightly. But I was founded by our Lord Himself to hand on His teaching, and He promised that He would be with me always, enabling me always to teach without error the truth revealed by Him. My credentials are plain and easy to understand. I offer you plain and simple proofs that I am the Teacher authorised by God, and that therefore you can trust me."

I proceed to examine these proofs, I am convinced by them, and I thankfully accept the Church's guidance. I know that I cannot trust my own private judgement to work out the answers to a multitude of complicated questions, over which all the Christian sects have disputed for nearly 1900 years. But I can trust it (with the grace of God to help me) to decide upon the plain and simple proofs offered by the Catholic Church that she has authority from our Lord to teach. What is ridiculous in that ? Is it ridi-

culous to say that I can trust my own judgement
to decide one very simple question, but that I
cannot trust it to decide a hundred very complicated questions ?

But next we are told that this acceptance of
the claims of the Catholic Church cannot be a
decision made once for all. " The continued
submission to it has to go on from day to day,
and the continued submission is simply a continued act of your own private judgement." It
is not quite clear what this means. But it seems
to mean that, having once accepted the claims
of the Catholic Church as true, you have to go on
accepting them, and in doing so you have still
nothing but your own private judgement to rely
upon. Even if this were true, it would not be a
very serious argument. Having once seen clearly
the truth of the Church's claims, there is no reason
why anyone should wish to be constantly going
back and reconsidering the decision. Once the
proofs have been clearly grasped, they are so
obvious that nobody wants to be continually
going over them again to assure himself of their
truth. And, indeed, the more thoroughly one
knows the Catholic Church from inside, the clearer
becomes the evidence for her Divine origin.

But in fact it is not true that after joining the
Church we have nothing but our own private

judgement to keep us steadfast in the decision once made. We have the gift of faith, which remains as a permanent supernatural " habit " in the soul. The initial act, indeed, by which we submitted to the Church's claims, involved a great deal more than a mere act of " private judgement," that is of the reason. The reason, indeed, had to decide on the evidence, but much more was involved. In fact the grace of God came first of all. It was grace that moved us to enquire, and it was grace that enlightened the reason to decide rightly. And then there was an act of the will to be made. The will, again moved by grace, had to decide to accept the Divine claim. So the initial act of Faith was made. But after that grace begins to work in a new way. God rewards this act of submission by a permanent gift of faith, which remains as an " infused virtue " in the soul. That is what gives us a permanent certainty, and makes it unnecessary to be continually renewing our initial act of private judgement. The gift of faith, once given, remains, unless we so abuse it by sinning against the light that God takes it away.

That is what explains what seems so strange a phenomenon to those outside, that, having once accepted the Faith, we retain an unshakable certainty and security. That is why we can repeat to those outside the confident invitation of Cardinal Newman : " Come to the [Catholic Church] as to your home, to the school of your souls, to the Mother of Saints, and to the vestibule of heaven. On the other hand, do not distress yourselves with thoughts whether, when you have joined her, your faith will last ; this is a suggestion of the enemy to hold you back. He who has begun a good work in you will perfect it ; He who has chosen you will be faithful to you ; put your cause into His hand, wait upon Him and you will surely persevere. . . . Take the experience of those who have gone before you in the same course ; they had many fears that their faith would fail them before taking the great step, but those fears vanished on their taking it ; they had fears, before they received the grace of faith, lest, after receiving it, they should lose it again, but no fears (except on the ground of their general frailness) after it was actually given."

CHAPTER IX

THE AUTHORITY OF THE CHURCH IN DOCTRINE

OUR authors now anticipate the very naturla criticism that they have destroyed the whole idea of a Church with authority to teach—the idea which from the time of the Oxford Movement was the whole basis of the "Anglo-Catholic" position, and distinguished it from that of what they called " Protestantism." They expect that Catholics will make the obvious comment : " But this is pure Protestantism ; where is the authority of the Church ? Do Anglo-Catholics at last realise that they have no room left for the authority which the Church has always claimed ? "

In fact, it is not " pure Protestantism," but something very much worse. The old Protestants did not believe in the authority of the Church, but they did believe in the authority of the Bible. They held this belief in a rather unintelligent way, but at least they had *some* authority. Messrs. Milner-White and Knox believe in none at all. It is not Protestantism but pure Rationalism. It is the negation of all belief in Revelation. Nevertheless they calmly answer,

" Not in the least." They really think that they
have " left room " for " the authority which the
Church has always claimed."

But if there is any fact of history which is
incontrovertible, it is that the authority which
the Church has always claimed is the right and
power to teach infallibly the truth revealed by
God. Between Catholics and the older " Anglo-
Catholics " that was common ground. The
difference between us was that we believe that
the Church, which has this authority, is one
undivided and indivisible Body, while they
maintained that it was split up into three sections.
But neither we nor they doubted that there was
a Church which had the right and the power to
teach infallibly. There was, therefore, no question about what the authority was which the
Church had always claimed. Now Messrs.
Milner-White and Knox wish to show that they
have still " left room " for this authority.

In fact, however, they do not attempt to prove
anything of the kind. They have already given
a new meaning to the word " authority "—a
meaning which is entirely their own.
" Authority," according to them, means " that
which gives us reason for believing." What they
therefore now try to show is not how, in spite of
their theories, they can still believe in a Church

which has authority to teach, in the accepted sense of the term, but how they can still find reasons for believing what they call "the Catholic Faith," although they have no teaching authority left.

The title of the chapter is therefore entirely misleading. We have not here to consider our authors' theory of a teaching authority, for they do not believe in any, but the reasons they give for still believing what they call "the Catholic Faith." These we must now proceed to examine.

But first we have to see what they mean by the "Catholic Faith." For this term also they use in a peculiar and original sense of their own. We are told that "in the actual course of history there have grown up two main forms of Christianity, the Catholic on the one hand, and the Protestant on the other. The two are perfectly clear and distinct types of religion. The Catholic type of religion may not be easy to define, but it is extremely easy to recognise. Its distinctive features are its insistence on the value of the sacramental life, on the need of an ordered ministry derived from the historic continuity of the episcopate with the Church of the Apostolic age, its tradition of mental prayer, and its belief in the living value of the communion of saints." And later on they say that " the Catholic Faith claims to be a system in the proper sense ; all its parts are connected with one another. You cannot safely or even reasonably say that you like some parts and propose to adopt them, but that you propose to leave out others because you do not like them."

They hold, then, that there is a connected system of doctrine, which is held by all " Catholics." And " Catholics " are all who practise a " type of religion " whose features are those described above. They include, therefore, all Roman Catholics, all the Eastern sects, " Orthodox," Nestorians, Monophysites, and so forth, and a certain number of Anglicans—not all Anglicans, but all those who are more or less High Church, all the various varieties and shades of " Anglo-Catholics." And yet we are told that there is one system of doctrine, so closely connected that you cannot reasonably accept some parts without accepting the whole, which is held by all these varieties of Christians. Of course it is manifest that nothing of the kind exists. There is, indeed, such a closely connected body of doctrine held by the Roman Catholic Church, but a " system " held in common by all the communities and groups mentioned only exists in the rather vivid imagination of Messrs. Milner-White and Knox.

However, we must go on to consider what they call the " authority," that is to say, their reasons for believing this non-existent system of doctrine. And in fact we find four different statements concerning this " authority." The statements contradict one another, but that is a trifle which does not disturb our authors.

1. The first of these statements is that " its authority lies in the fact that where men and women are prepared to accept it and give it a fair trial they will find that it produces in their lives the finest fruits of Christian holiness." This can only mean that all those communities, or sections of communities, that have bishops, insist on the value of sacraments, and pray to the Saints and for the dead, produce fruits of holiness which are conspicuously superior to those produced by any communities or groups of Christians which have no bishops, or attach less importance to the sacraments, or do not pray to the Saints or for the dead. (I leave out the question of " mental prayer," because that is a practice not peculiar to any particular section or sections.) Unfortunately this is not manifest at all. I have found no evidence at all that the High Church people in the Church of England are holier than the old-fashioned Evangelicals. In fact, I think that the reverse is true. Still less,

after four years residence in the Near East, am I convinced that the motley crowd of adherents of the Oriental sects are markedly holier than many good Protestants. In this case, in fact, I am quite certain that the reverse is not only true, but obvious to all who have lived in the Near East.

2. A little later, however, we find another " authority," namely, " its claim to provide a rational account of the nature of God and of His dealings with men." As a supplementary argument for the truth of the real Catholic Faith, that is to say the perfectly coherent body of doctrine taught by the Roman Catholic Church, this is perfectly valid. That is to say that it goes to confirm the other main proofs that it is a Divine Revelation. But how such a claim can be maintained for anything so shadowy as a vague something supposed to be the common teaching of the Catholic Church, all the Eastern sects and several varieties of Anglicans, it is difficult to see.

But this is of the less importance, since again a little later it is admitted that these two " authorities " do not guarantee the truth of anything in particular. " The Church," we are told, " has behind her the experience of the ages to show that the system taken as a whole is true, and it is only reasonable for her to say that if you believe something like seven-tenths of the whole, you ought to be prepared to accept the other three-tenths. But the Church has no right to say this unless she is prepared also to give you her reasons for thinking that the parts whose value you do not see are really true." So in fact all the doctrines have to be proved one by one in some other way, which is not described. And yet we have been told that there *are* no other reasons for believing anything except the two given above. This is all very puzzling.

3. But we go on to the next statement. "The only authority in the Catholic Church which can ultimately preserve the truth is the power of the Holy Ghost to guide theologians *in the end*[1] to a true understanding of the Faith." And again: "There seems no reason to be afraid that He will not *in the end*[1] guide the Church into the truth. It may seem that some writers have gone very far wrong in their search. If so, we should have sufficient faith to believe that He will *reveal*[1] the fact that their teachings are wrong as He has always done in the past."

Remembering that, in our authors' terminology, "authority" means "that which gives us reasons for believing," the statement amounts to this. The reason for believing some vague thing called the Catholic Faith, which nobody can

[1] Italics are mine.

define, is a hope that *in the end*[1] theologians will
find out the truth, and that some day we shall
have a new revelation to show which of the many
contradictory doctrines advanced by contending
theologians to-day is right. Indeed, it seems a
very good reason for believing nothing at all;
for as yet, according to this theory, there is
nothing for us to believe. We have to wait until
the Holy Ghost has guided the theologians, who
are now groping in the dark and quarrelling
among themselves, to the truth, and has revealed
which of them are right and which are wrong.

4. But after all this we rather unexpectedly
come upon quite a different "authority." The
authors suddenly remember that there are
Creeds, and tell us that "Anglo-Catholics possess
in the Creeds and in the living tradition of the
practice of the Catholic Faith all the authority
that any other body possesses, so far as the
foundation of the faith is concerned." I pass
over the fact that in the Church of England everybody is free to interpret the Creeds as he likes,
and that the extreme Low Church and Broad
Church parties profess to believe in the same
Creeds as the "Anglo-Catholics," only explaining
them quite differently, and there is nobody to
say which is right, so that the "Anglo-Catholics"

---

[1] Italics are mine.

have no more authority for their doctrines in the Creeds than those whom they call "extreme Protestants." But whence do the Creeds get their authority? They did not fall down from heaven ready made. Their authority is precisely that of the Church which drew them up or authorised them. But Messrs. Milner-White and Knox have already denied that the Church has or ever had any real authority to define the Faith. Therefore the Creeds for them are nothing but statements of doctrine, which everybody must judge for himself, and perfectly valueless as authorities, even in the sense given to that term by our authors. In themselves, and apart from the authority of an infallible teaching Church, they cannot give reasons for believing anything.

Let us now sum up the situation. Messrs. Milner-White and Knox have quite clearly abandoned all idea of a Church teaching with authority in any intelligible sense of the term. According to them there never was such a Church, and there ought not to be. The Church ought to let everybody teach what he likes. Bishops would only "make themselves ridiculous" if they attempted to excommunicate heretics. Having abandoned this idea, they attempt to substitute some other reasons for believing some vague thing called "the Catholic Faith," which cannot

be defined. But these reasons amount to nothing.
On their principles I can see no reasonable
grounds for believing anything.

But in fact they have gone further than that.
They have really abandoned the whole idea of
Revelation, as that term has always been understood. They clearly do not believe that any
definite truths have been revealed. The truth
about God and our relation to Him has to be found
out by our own efforts in the same way as the
truth about the material world has to be discovered. This is made clear by the note at the
bottom of page 93. There we are told that the
argument for the necessity of an infallible
teacher, if we are to have any clear knowledge
of the truth revealed by God, is " rubbish."
And to show that it is " rubbish " a supposed
parallel is taken from the practice of medicine.
We are told that, on our principles, unless there
is an " Infallible Living Voice in medicine,"
nobody will know how to get his diseases cured.
But the methods of curing diseases are found out
by research and experiment. Consequently, if
there is any force in the parallel, it must mean
that in the matter of our eternal salvation God
has revealed nothing, and the way to eternal life
can only be found out by methods similar to
those of medical science, and for nineteen

hundred years Christians have been entirely deluded in supposing that they have any revelation on the matter.

Our authors, however, once more try to show that anyhow the Catholic Church can provide nothing more certain than their own vague speculations. It seems unnecessary to go into these arguments, because they are nothing but a repetition of what they have already said, the paradoxical argument that the Catholic Church has never really defined anything as *de fide*. I have already dealt sufficiently with this. There are just one or two remarks on which it seems worth while to comment.

We are told that if there were an Infallible Voice, " it would be its duty to lay down infallibly the solution of all sorts of modern problems." Why ? Did our Lord say to His Church, " Go and teach all nations how to solve all the problems of all sorts that will ever arise " ? No, He told His Church to teach them the way to eternal life, which He had revealed, and that is what the Catholic Church, and the Catholic Church alone, does to-day with clearness and certainty.

Again, we are told that " the discoveries of scientists such as Darwin proved that the literal historical truth of the account of creation in Genesis could no longer be maintained. The majority of English Bishops denounced the scientists. So did the majority of English Protestants. The Vatican Council seemed to do so by declaring the divine authorship of the Scriptures and the necessity of interpreting them as the Church has always done."

Messrs. Milner-White and Knox really ought to know better than this. They ought to know that the Catholic Church has never held that the early chapters of Genesis are all to be interpreted literally, and certainly the Vatican Council did not say so. There have been many ways of interpreting them from S Augustine downwards. They say that " the Infallible Voice of the Church ought to have been able to declare precisely in what sense, if any, the old view of the Bible must be altered. It has never done so." No, and it never will. The Catholic Church will never change its teaching that the Holy Scriptures, being written under the inspiration of the Holy Ghost, " have God for their Author," and therefore contain no error. The interpretation of various passages is a matter for scholars, with the authority of the Church to warn them against such interpretations as are contrary to the Faith. It is the business of the Church to guard the Faith, not to provide ready-made solutions of all critical problems.

CHAPTER X

THE AUTHORITY OF THE CHURCH IN MORALS

THE first objection made in "One God and Father of All" to the Church's claim to be an infallible guide in morals is one that we should not have expected from anyone who had seriously studied the meaning of the claim. "If it is admitted," they say, "that the infallibility of the Pope does not safeguard him from personal moral failure, it is very hard to see how it can safeguard him from making mistakes in moral questions." In fact, to any person of average intelligence, it is very easy to see. The Papal prerogative of infallibility means that God so guides the Pope that when, using his supreme power as Pastor and Teacher of all Christians, he defines a doctrine concerning faith or morals to be held by the whole Church, he does not err. In those cases the power of God prevents him from making a mistake. Our authors will have it that that is impossible unless the Pope is impeccable. They must have very odd ideas about the power of God. According to them it is difficult to see how God could prevent Alexander VI from giving a wrong definition. One is tempted to ask what sort of God they believe in, if He cannot do so simple a thing as that.

But the main arguments against the infallible authority of the Church in morals are two. The first is that there is no need for any such authority, because everybody's conscience tells them what is right and what is wrong without their having to be taught. The other is the same old argument that they have used against its infallibility in Faith, that the Church has never made any infallible pronouncement. Let us examine these two objections.

There is no need, we are told, for such a teacher. " In most matters we do not need the authority of the Church to teach us. Our authority is the voice of conscience, revealing to us what is sometimes called the Natural Law. This law, as interpreted by the teaching of our Lord, is perfectly clear and obvious in its main principles. It is the law by which ordinary men and women live, even though they do not profess to be Christians. . . . It may sometimes be necessary for the Church to teach ignorant people, living in very low moral surroundings, that certain actions are obviously wrong. It may have to teach savages that polygamy is wrong, or it may have to teach people who are Christians in name that, for instance, fornication is wrong. But the Church must do so by showing them that such sins are contrary to what their own conscience shows them to be right."

Here we notice first that the restricted function of teaching allowed to the Church is a very odd one. It is only necessary to instruct ignorant people living in very low moral surroundings. But it is not really necessary even in their case. Or rather the Church does not really *teach* them anything. It only shows them that polygamy, fornication and so forth are contrary to what their own conscience shows them to be right. In other words, it only shows them what their own conscience has already shown them, which seems to be a rather unnecessary proceeding.

It is, of course, quite true that the Natural Law is made known to us by the voice of conscience. But Messrs. Milner-White and Knox must have a very small experience of human nature if they think that the uninstructed conscience of every individual is an infallible guide. It is precisely one of the unfortunate consequences of original sin that men, swayed by unruly passions and desires, are unable to use their consciences rightly. It is not merely that they desire to do things that they know to be wrong, but they are actually blinded, so that they cannot judge rightly. It is because of this that they do need an external guide to fall back upon. It is a matter of common experience.

But perhaps our opponents would reply that it is sufficient for the individual to fall back upon the general conscience of the community. Would that it were so! It is true that in Europe a fairly accurate code of morals is still generally accepted, at least in theory. But that is only because for a thousand years Europe was taught by the Catholic Church. When at the Reformation a large part of Europe abandoned the Catholic Faith, which it had been taught by the Church, it did not at once abandon the Catholic code of morals, although there was a great falling away in practice. And even now those large numbers of people who have given up all profession of Christianity still for the most part accept in theory the traditional ethics. But there are increasing signs that that will not continue much longer. One of the most alarming phenomena of the present age is its deliberate questioning of the fundamental laws of right and wrong. For example, it is only the other day that a French jury justified a young man, who had deliberately murdered his mother, in order to put an end to her suffering, and there were numerous letters in the English newspapers applauding their action. The Divine law of marriage has long since been thrown overboard, as our divorce courts testify. The murder of unborn children is justified by many. And Messrs. Milner-White and Knox themselves are badly in need of instruction on the subject of contraception.

The next argument is that, however desirable an infallible guide may be, the Catholic Church is useless for the purpose, because it has never given any infallible pronouncement on a question of morals.

This is no doubt in accordance with our authors' theory that at most only two infallible decisions have been given in the whole history of the Church. I have already dealt with that, and need not do so again here. But there is another strange misunderstanding. They seem to imagine that the Church never teaches anything clearly and certainly until there has been an actual definition by the Pope. They forget that the Church only defines a doctrine in that way when it has been disputed, or when some serious doubt has arisen. And by this I mean, of course, when the question or doubt has arisen within the Church; for if the teaching of the

Church is perfectly clear there is no need of a solemn definition to deal with those outside. Also there must be a really serious doubt, and one that is so persistent that it cannot be dealt with in other and simpler ways. A solemn definition is only employed as a last resort, when the doubt has become so serious that it must be finally settled. And in moral questions such doubts within the Church very seldom arise. The Church's moral system is being more and more questioned by those outside, as I have said, but within the Church there is no question. There is no need for the Church to define that murder is a sin, because no Catholic doubts it or has questioned it. And this answers the objection about contraception. There is no more need for the Church solemnly to define that it is a sin than for it to define that adultery is a sin.

It would be interesting to know who the " some Roman Catholics " are who " argue as though the reason why [contraception] is wrong is that the Roman Church forbids it," and that " if the Roman Church were to sanction it, it would cease to be wrong." It is, no doubt, possible that some very ignorant Catholic may have talked in that way, but he must have been very ignorant indeed. Any Catholic, who is not crassly ignorant, knows perfectly well the distinction between the

Divine Law, which the Church has power to teach and explain infallibly, but cannot alter by one hair's breadth, and Ecclesiastical Law, which, being made by the Church, the Church can change. It would indeed be crass ignorance to suppose that a moral vice could be the subject of an ecclesiastical prohibition only.

Messrs. Milner-White and Knox show strange ignorance of the Catholic practice of the Confessional when they try to make out that " it allows wide loop-holes " for the practice of this detestable vice. They seem to have got hold of a certain answer of the Sacred Penitentiary, which they have entirely failed to understand. The Sacred Penitentiary does say that if a confessor has a well-grounded suspicion that one of his penitents has been committing this sin, he ought as a rule prudently and discreetly to question him. But it does *not* give as " one of the reasons which permit him to make exceptions the principle that he should not refuse absolution to a sinner who is in the habit of relapsing into mortal sin, if he has serious reasons for fearing that the effect of his refusal will be to drive the sinner away entirely from the use of the sacraments." Such a principle is unknown in the Catholic Church, and that for the very good reason that the Church never refuses absolution merely on the ground that the unhappy man " is in the habit of relapsing into mortal sin." It would, indeed, be a most uncharitable thing to do. The whole question is whether he shows sufficient signs of contrition. But of course there are cases in which it would not be wise to ask questions. Questioning a penitent is a very delicate matter, and one that requires great prudence on the part of the confessor. But to say that confessors are not encouraged to question the penitent on every occasion, after the manner of a barrister cross-examining a witness, does not imply that the Church " allows wide loop-holes " for this or any other sin.

As an illustration of this leaving of wide loop-holes we find this : " The drawback of the Roman position is that if a married couple really feel that they are justified in using methods of birth control and do not confess it (which they need not do, if they do not believe that they are sinning), and if their confessor thinks it wiser not to ask, they are being left to their own judgement in a matter where they really need unprejudiced advice." In other words, if a penitent does not know that contraception is sinful (which in the case of a Catholic is very unlikely), and therefore does not confess it, he will probably go on doing it. So that, when

Messrs. Milner-White and Knox talk about the Church " leaving wide loop-holes," they mean that, although the Church clearly condemns this sin, it is not able to ensure that every one of its members shall be accurately instructed in the matter. And that is said to be " not a dignified position for a society which claims to speak with a voice which is divine and cannot err " !

CHAPTER XI

ANGLICAN ORDERS

MR. JOHNSON, in "One Lord, One Faith," does not go at any length into the question of Anglican Orders. It is quite a secondary question. For, even if Anglican Orders were valid, Anglicans would be no more Catholics than they are now. When Mr. Johnson had come to see that the Roman Catholic Church is the one true Church of God, he naturally accepted its ruling on the question of Anglican Orders without any detailed investigation. But, as Messrs. Milner-White and Knox make this the occasion for another attack on the Catholic Church, with two prominent sub-headings, "The Error of Pope Eugenius" and "The Blunder of Leo XIII," they must be answered.

It is not quite obvious why Eugenius IV is dragged in at all, except as another supposed illustration of the unreliability of the Infallible Authority. Our authors quote the well-known *Decretum pro Armenis*, in which that Pontiff says, among other things, that the "matter" in the Sacrament of Orders is the "tradition of the instruments," and the "form" is : "Receive power to offer sacrifice in the Church for the living and the dead." They then proceed to say that this is obviously wrong, because it is certain that there was no "tradition of the instruments" for many centuries, and so here is another bad mistake of the Infallible Authority. And they end with their customary gibe that Roman theologians "get out of it by that 'ordinary authority' which the Pope is supposed to have been using whenever he is proved to have made a mistake."

The answer is twofold. In the first place it is not quite so obvious, as our authors suppose, that Eugenius made a mistake. Many theologians hold that our Lord did not determine the matter of each sacrament *specifice*, but only *generice*. That is to say, that He gave to the Apostles a general notion of the signs to be employed, but did not in every case determine them more exactly, leaving it to the Church to do so. Now it is admitted that from the beginning the essential action in conferring Orders was the imposition of hands. But it is also clear that the "tradition of the instruments" is only a fuller expression of the power thus conferred. The Church has, it is true, no power to change the essential constituents in the matter and form of the sacraments, but it is quite at liberty to amplify the external expression of the form. This is what the Church has done in adding the tradition of the instruments. And, as this became a traditional usage in the Roman Church, it is obvious that any Church desirous, as the Armenians were, of full union with the Roman Church could rightly be asked to adopt this additional rite. And that is all that Eugenius did. Is it credible that he meant to imply that the imposition of hands was no longer to be regarded as essential ?

But the most important thing is that both the circumstances and the wording of the *Decretum pro Armenis* show that the Pope had no intention of " defining a doctrine concerning faith or morals to be held by the whole Church." It was not the basis of the reconciliation of the Armenians. The negotiations had been already concluded, and then, in order that the Armenians might be further instructed in the method of administering the sacraments in accordance with the usage of the Roman Church, the Pope sent them this instruction. There is no indication that it is a definition solemnly laid down for the whole Church to accept. It is surely very easy to see the difference between this and such a document, for example, as the Bull *Exsurge*

Domine condemning the heresies of Luther, in which the Pope says : " By the authority of Almighty God and of the Blessed Apostles Peter and Paul and Our own We condemn and reprobate all the aforesaid articles or errors, collectively and singly, as being respectively (according as is indicated) heretical or scandalous or false, and We decree and declare that they are to be considered by all the Faithful of either sex as condemned, reprobated and rejected." Messrs. Milner-White and Knox may call this " special pleading " if they like, but most people of ordinary intelligence will call it common sense.

We proceed to " the blunder of Leo XIII." It is well known that from the time of Queen Mary the Catholic Church has consistently treated Anglican Orders as null and void, and has always ordained without condition ex-Anglican ministers who have become Catholics and were to be promoted to the Priesthood. At the end of the nineteenth century, however, certain French priests, who had become friendly with some members of the " Anglo-Catholic " party in the Church of England, raised the question of their validity in such a way that it was thought desirable to have it examined afresh. A Commission was appointed and went into the evidence at great length. The evidence was then pre-

K

sented to the Holy Office. The Cardinals composing that Congregation considered it all with the greatest care, and came to the unanimous conclusion that Anglican Orders were invalid. Then the Pope, who had presided at the last meeting of the Congregation, issued the Bull *Apostolicæ Curæ*, in which he renews the declarations of his predecessors, that " ordinations carried out according to the Anglican rite have been, and are, absolutely null and utterly void."

But almost immediately some of the French supporters of Anglican Orders began to write that this was not a definitive decision, and that before long the Holy See would be obliged to change its position. And so finally the Pope wrote to the Archbishop of Paris to say that it had been his intention " to judge [the question] absolutely, and settle it definitely," and that he had done it " with such a weight of arguments, such clearness, and such authority in the form, that no man of prudence and good faith could bring his sentence again into discussion, and that all Catholics must accept it with full obedience, as being *perpetuo ratam, firmam, irrevocabilem.*"

Against this our authors first attempt to dispute the fact that the Catholic Church has always regarded Anglican Orders as invalid. The best way to examine this contention is to put down first the undisputed facts, and then the arguments by which Messrs. Milner-White and Knox try to refute the evidence.

The undisputed facts, then, are these:

1. Immediately after the accession of Mary the English Bishops had no hesitation in regarding the Orders conferred by means of the Edwardine Ordinal as invalid, and proceeded to ordain to the Priesthood such of the ministers as they considered fit. The reason is clearly given in a decree of Queen Mary dated March 4, 1554, in which she describes the persons who require ordination as " such persons as were heretofore promoted to any Orders after the new sort and fashion of Order, considering they were not ordained in very deed."

2. Although Cardinal Pole did not arrive until later, Mary had been in correspondence with him from the autumn of 1553, and there can be no doubt that what was then done was done after consultation with him.

3. There is a letter of Pope Julius III to Cardinal Pole dated March 8, 1554, renewing and enlarging the powers conferred on him by a previous letter of August 5, 1553, in which explicit directions are given for the ordination of those who had not been properly ordained. The Pope gives faculties to Cardinal Pole to

KI

absolve all persons from heresy, and to grant to
priests " dispensation from all irregularity that
they may have incurred, so that, provided that
before their lapse into heresy they had been
rightly and lawfully promoted or ordained, they
might minister even in the ministry of the altar,
and that in cases where they had not been so
promoted they might now be promoted to all
the orders, including sacred orders and the
priesthood, by their own ordinaries, provided
they were found to be worthy and fitting
subjects."

4. The Holy See had been in possession of a
copy of the Edwardine Ordinal since June, 1549,
so that the Pope knew the nature of it, and,
when he speaks of those who had not been
properly ordained, he can only refer to those
ordained according to that rite.

5. Cardinal Pole ratified all the actions taken
by the Bishops before his arrival, including the
ordinations. He therefore manifestly approved
of their action in that matter.

6. There are letters of Cardinal Pole to various
Bishops, sub-delegating his authority to them,
granting them power, among other things, to dispense priests " from all irregularity they may
have incurred through receiving Orders from
heretical and schismatical Bishops, and other-

wise not altogether rightly, *provided always that in their ordination the form and intention of the Church was preserved.*"

7. There is definite evidence of the ordination of two ministers to the priesthood after the coming of Pole, and, therefore, with his authority

8. There is the Bull of Pope Paul IV, *Præclara Carissimi*, dated June 20, 1555, ratifying all the acts of Cardinal Pole, and renewing his power to dispense priests from irregularity, " provided always that those who have been promoted to major as well as minor ecclesiastical orders by any other person than a Bishop or an Archbishop duly and rightly ordained shall be bound to receive the said Orders anew from their ordinary, and shall not in the meantime minister in the said Orders."

9. There is a further letter from Paul IV to Cardinal Pole, explaining more fully the meaning of the above Bull, in which he says that " it is only those Bishops and Archbishops who were *not ordained and consecrated in the form of the Church* that cannot be said to be duly and rightly ordained, and therefore *the persons promoted by them to these Orders have not received Orders,* but ought and are bound to receive anew the said Orders from their ordinary according to the tenor of our aforesaid letters."

10. From that time onwards many hundreds of Anglican ministers have been converted to the Faith, and those who were promoted to the Priesthood have always been ordained unconditionally and without question.

Against all these facts Messrs. Milner-White and Knox make the following allegations :

1. That eight ministers ordained according to the Edwardine Ordinal were not deprived of their benefices in the reign of Mary, and there is no evidence of their having been re-ordained.

2. That four who were deprived were deprived not for lack of valid Orders but for being married.

3. That although we know of fifteen who were certainly re-ordained there is a large number of whom nothing is known. Some probably fled to the Continent, but *it seems likely*[1] that many remained, and of their re-ordination there is no trace.

4. Only two ministers were, so far as we know, re-ordained after the coming of Pole, and therefore he " seems to have regarded re-ordination as unnecessary." A footnote improves on this by transforming this surmise, without further evidence, into the definite assertion that Cardinal Pole did not regard Anglican Orders as invalid.

[1] Italics are mine.

And so the conclusion is that the Roman Church has not always done so. It was only " later Roman practice " that " decided on re-ordination."

Of these allegations the second proves nothing. It does not follow that if they had not been married they would have been allowed to say Mass without re-ordination. The fact of other re-ordinations indicates the contrary. The third is mere unfounded guessing. The fourth proves nothing. The most probable explanation of the fewness of the re-ordinations after the coming of Pole is that there were not many more of the Edwardine ministers who were fit and proper persons for the Priesthood.

The only fact, therefore, that creates the slightest difficulty is that eight ministers do not seem to have been deprived of their benefices, and there is no record of their ordination. But the mere fact of their not being deprived would not in itself prove that their Orders were recognised as valid. We do not know what particular circumstances there may have been that made it difficult to get rid of them. And in any case this is of very little weight against all the positive evidence that re-ordination was insisted on by the English Bishops, Cardinal Pole and the Pope himself.

We are next informed that " it is matter of common knowledge that the condemnation of Anglican Orders by Pope Leo XIII was not due to the opinion of experts but to the pressure of English Roman Catholics, who felt that the position of the Roman Church in its attempt to win over Anglo-Catholics would be stronger if they could proclaim that the Pope had condemned Anglican Orders."

Not only is this not " matter of common knowledge," but it is entirely contrary to the facts, as may be seen by anyone who takes the trouble to read Snead-Cox's " Life of Cardinal Vaughan," Vol. II, chapter vi, and Cardinal Gasquet's " Leaves from my Diary." There they will see clearly enough that it was simply a question of the overwhelming evidence, which so convinced first the entire Congregation of the Holy Office, and then the Pope himself, that they had no alternative but to declare them invalid.

Incidentally, why should English Roman Catholics be so anxious to have Anglican Orders declared invalid ? Far from helping in the conversion of " Anglo-Catholics," it is one of the difficulties. They often find it hard to be obliged to acknowledge that they have never really received our Lord's Body and Blood, when they thought that they did. It is an unreasonable attitude, but it is very common. Consequently, it would actually make things easier for us if we could admit their validity. It is only hard facts that compel us to deny it.

Our authors, however, now proceed to attack the arguments of *Apostolicae Curae*. But in doing so they make some astonishing statements. First they tell us that at the Reformation the English Church " neither affirmed nor denied the existence of a sacrifice." But what are the facts ?

1. It was the avowed object of all the Protestant leaders above all things to get rid of the Sacrifice of the Mass. Here are a few of their statements :

Cranmer wrote : " The greatest blasphemy and injury that can be against Christ, and yet universally used throughout the popish kingdom, is this, that the priests make their Mass a sacrifice propitiatory, to remit the sins as well of themselves as of others, both quick and dead, to whom they list to apply the same. . . . Nor Christ never did this honour to any creature, that he should make a sacrifice of Him, nor did not ordain the Sacrament of His Holy Supper, to the intent that either the priest or the people should sacrifice Christ again, or that the priests should make a sacrifice of Him for the people ; but His Holy Supper was ordained for this purpose, that every man, eating and drinking thereof, should remember that Christ died for him, and should so exercise his faith, and comfort himself by the remembrance of Christ's benefits, and so give unto Christ most hearty thanks and give himself also clearly unto Him."

Ridley wrote : " They pluck away the honour from the only sacrifice of Christ whilst this Sacrament and Mass-sacrifice is believed to be propitiatory, and such a one as purgeth the souls, both of the quick and the dead." And again : " All that intend to be partakers of life and salvation with Christ in His Kingdom ought to abhor and abstain from the popish Mass now set up by Satan and Antichrist in England again." And so he says that altars ought to be pulled down and tables substituted, because " the form of a table shall more move the simple from the superstitious opinions of the popish Mass unto the right use of the Lord's Supper. For the use of an altar is to make a sacrifice upon it ; the use of a table is to serve for men to eat upon."

Hooper wrote : " The Papists offer neither Christ nor a sacrifice in their Masses, but a detestable idol. For Christ Himself, in the true substance and personality of our nature, sacrificed to God once for all on the Cross ; and now, since He liveth and dieth now no more so no more, either by Himself or by another, is He offered for the redemption of sins."

The quotations might be multiplied indefinitely.

2. In compiling the new Book of Common Prayer out of the old service books they deliberately cut out all reference to sacrifice. For example, in the Sarum Missal, used in England before the Reformation, occur such expressions as these :

" Receive, O holy Trinity, this oblation, which I, an unworthy sinner, offer in Thy honour, Blessed Mary's and all the Saints ; for my sins and offences ; for the salvation of the living, and the repose of all the faithful departed. In the name of the Father and of the Son, and of the Holy Ghost, let this new sacrifice be acceptable to Almighty God."

" Brethren and sisters, pray for me that my sacrifice and yours may alike be accepted by the Lord our God."

" We beseech Thee, O Lord, look graciously upon this present sacrifice, whereby being purified we may take part in Thy Son's Nativity." (From one of the Secrets for Advent.)

The Missal is full of expressions of that kind.

And then in the ordination of priests according to the old Pontifical we have : " Receive power to offer sacrifice to God, and to celebrate Mass for the living and the dead," and " May the blessing of Almighty God, the Father, the Son and the Holy Ghost descend upon you that you may offer acceptable sacrifices for the sins and offences of the people unto Almighty God," and so forth.

All such expressions were deliberately cut out. Now, deliberately to cut out such things does not indicate an attitude of neutrality. It shows that they wished to get rid of the doctrine, and is equivalent to a denial of it. You might as well say that the French anti-clericals who cut out the name of God from their schoolbooks " took a moderate line," and " neither affirmed nor denied " His existence.

3. Article XXXI of the XXXIX Articles says : " The sacrifices of Masses in the which it was commonly said that the priest did offer Christ for the quick and the dead, to have remission of pain or guilt, were blasphemous fables and dangerous deceits."

4. In order to make it quite clear to everybody that the Sacrifice of the Mass had been abolished, and the " Lord's Supper " substituted for it, it was ordered that all the old altars be removed,

and wooden tables substituted for them. Often
the old altar stone was put in the pavement,
in order that everybody might tread on it. In
other cases it was broken and thrown out.

But next we come to a statement which is
really original in its audacity. We are solemnly
informed that in thus " neither affirming nor
denying the existence of a sacrifice " the Church
of England " did not ignore any formal doctrine
of the Church, for no such doctrine existed." We
are actually asked to believe that in the beginning
of the sixteenth century no doctrine of the
Sacrifice of the Mass existed in the Catholic
Church !

If I had not read this statement in plain
print I should not have believed it possible that
any sane person could make it. But after a little
reflection it becomes clear what our friends are
driving at. They cannot get rid of the strange
idea that no doctrine is taught by the Church
until it has been defined. If this doctrine was
not defined until the Council of Trent, it was
because until then nobody had denied it. The
most superficial student of history knows perfectly well that at the beginning of the sixteenth
century it was the universal and undisputed
teaching of the Church that the Mass is a sacrifice. The quotations from the Missal and the

Pontifical quoted above are alone enough to prove it. So is the quotation from Cranmer that it was " universally used throughout the popish kingdom." Cranmer had himself been a Catholic priest, and knew very well what he was talking about. But it is hardly necessary to labour this point, for it is hardly credible that anyone will take it seriously.

But the most interesting thing to notice here is that these gentlemen, who loudly proclaim that they are " Catholics," and can be easily seen to have essentially the same religion as Roman Catholics and the Eastern " Orthodox," and to be quite distinct from Protestants, tell us that the doctrine that the Mass is a sacrifice is no part of the Faith. They hold that it was unknown in the Apostolic Church, that it was just " a gradual development of Christian devotion," that " it was only formulated in the course of centuries," and that the belief grew up only because " Catholic devotion had always *felt* that the Mass is a sacrifice."

There seems to be a little contradiction here. How had " Catholic devotion *always* felt that the Mass is a sacrifice " if nobody had any idea of it for the first few centuries ? Was the Church not Catholic from the beginning ? And, if not, when did it become Catholic ? But could there be a clearer proof that our authors have not only thrown overboard the whole basis of the " Anglo-Catholic " position, but have ceased to attempt to show any reasonable grounds for their position at all ? It all comes to this. You like a certain type of devotion, which is more or less similar to that of the Catholic Church. If you practise that type of devotion you *feel* that the Mass is a sacrifice. And there is nothing more to be said.

But, if that is so, it does not seem to matter much whether Anglican ministers have valid Orders, or any sort of Orders. If a Wesleyan minister took it into his head to practise the " Catholic type of religion," and persuaded his flock to do the same, no doubt they could produce the proper kind of feelings, and so they would have a true Mass and a true sacrifice.

Still, for the sake of those readers of " One God and Father of All " who do not go to the same lengths of Modernism as its authors, we may examine their attempt to refute the Bull. Their arguments are two. The first is that " although the English Ordinal did not specify the purpose of the priesthood in so far as the offering of the Eucharistic Sacrifice is concerned . . . the Ordinal itself makes it amply clear that the duties of the priesthood include the administration of the Sacraments, including the Eucharist." And the second is that " the doctrine of intention " put forward in the Bull is all wrong, because it is " the view of Leo XIII that for the valid giving of Orders you must include a definite intention and mention of conferring some power which the Church in later ages has come to regard as an important part of the priestly office."

Now, the two grounds on which Leo XIII judged Anglican Orders to be invalid were " defect of form " and " defect of intention."

It is well known that the Sacraments, being sensible and efficient signs of invisible grace, must somehow signify the grace which they effect. For this purpose it is necessary to use, in conjunction with the material sign, some form of words which will make clear its purpose. For example, the imposition of hands is used both in Confirmation and Ordination. By itself, therefore, it is not sufficiently definite. Some form of words must be used in conjunction with it which makes clear the purpose of the imposition. This is what is technically called the " form."

Now, in the Sacrament of Orders the form may vary, and does vary considerably in different rites. But it must somehow signify clearly that the purpose of this particular imposition of hands is to convey the grace and power of the Priesthood. And this the form used in the Edwardine Ordinal did not do. There is no mention of priesthood, or of the essential power of the priesthood, which is the power to offer sacrifice. The form was : " Receive the Holy Ghost ; whose sins thou dost forgive they are forgiven ; and whose sins thou dost retain they are retained. And be thou a faithful dispenser of the Word of God, and of His holy Sacraments ; in the name of the Father and of the Son and of the Holy Ghost. Amen." The words of the present Ordinal, " for the office and work of a Priest in the Church of God," were only inserted in 1662. The Anglican authorities seemed by that time to have realised the defect of the form, and to have made this effort to improve it. But, unfortunately, it was a hundred years too late.

The " doctrine of intention put forward in the Bull " bears no resemblance to the travesty of it which Messrs. Milner-White and Knox give. To show this it is only necessary to quote the Pope's words : " The Church does not judge about the mind and intention, in so far as it is something by its nature internal ; but in so far as it is manifested externally she is bound to judge concerning it. When anyone has rightly

L

and seriously made use of the due form and matter requisite for effecting or conferring the Sacrament, he is considered by that very fact to do what the Church does. On this principle rests the doctrine that a Sacrament is truly conferred by the ministry of one who is a heretic or unbaptised,[1] provided the Catholic rite is employed. On the other hand, if the rite be changed, with the manifest intention of introducing another rite not approved by the Church and of rejecting what, by the institution of Christ, belongs to the nature of the Sacrament, then it is clear that not only is the necessary intention wanting to the Sacrament, but that the intention is adverse to and destructive of the Sacrament." That seems to be so plain as to need no comment.

But notice again how, in their anxiety to prove the foolishness of Leo XIII, Messrs. Milner-White and Knox have abandoned the whole "Anglo-Catholic" position. For, according to them, our Lord did not institute a sacrificing priesthood. The power to offer sacrifice is only one "which the Church in later ages has come to regard as an important part of the priestly office." In other words Messrs. Milner-White

---

[1] In the case of the unbaptised this, of course, only refers to the administration of baptism.

and Knox do not even claim to have valid Orders in the Catholic sense, for they do not believe that our Lord instituted a sacrificing priesthood. They think that that was only an idea that grew up in later ages. That is to say that our Lord did not institute any priesthood at all. Then why all this bother about Orders ?

The rest of the chapter need not detain us long. It is argued that the chaotic condition of the Church of England is no reason for leaving it, and this on two grounds. The first is that the Roman Church is just as bad, because at one time there were two Popes. The answer is, of course, that there never were two Popes and there could not be. There were two, and at one time three, claimants to the Papacy, but only one of them was the Pope. Many people were misled and attached themselves to the anti-popes, just as at an earlier time many unfortunate Orientals were misled and followed Photius into schism. But how do such incidents prove that the Church is not one and undivided ? All that happened was that those who followed the anti-pope were temporarily separated from the Church. That was unfortunate for them, but it is difficult to see how it affects us.

It does not seem necessary to answer mere mud-throwing, such as the talk about our

" quite unscrupulous zeal for converts," and " a common Roman attitude," which is " quite content to ignore the millions who are without God in this world and direct its energies entirely to securing proselytes from Anglicanism." The only answer to these things is that they are not true. Since we believe that the Catholic Church is the one true Church of God, we naturally seek to bring into it everyone who will come, whether they be Anglicans, Baptists, Jews or Atheists. And, in fact, a very large proportion of those who are annually received into the Church are people who previously had no very definite religion of any any kind. Indeed, I should say, judging from my own experience, that they are the great majority.

Finally, we have an appeal to unreasoning emotion. It is suggested that the " difficulties " in the Church of England are the " cross " that Anglicans are called upon to bear, and that therefore it is wrong to try to escape from them by joining the " Roman " Church. It is a specious argument, but it misses the whole point. It is not difficulties and trials, or the hope of finding life easier in the Catholic Church, that makes people leave the Church of England. (Indeed it is not very worthy of any Christian ministers to make such a suggestion of one whom they describe as " an old and intimate friend " of one of

them, and " a revered acquaintance " of the
other.) What has made so many of us leave the
Church of England is the conviction that a
Church which teaches nothing definite, but
leaves its ministers to teach what they please,
cannot be the Church instituted by Christ, with
a commission to teach the truth revealed by
Him, and a promise that it will always do so.

A curious footnote begs waverers to take
courage because of the " vast progress " made by
" Anglo-Catholics " since the beginning of the
Oxford Movement. The evidence of this progress
is that clergymen are no longer sent to prison for
wearing vestments, and that some of the Bishops
are now even tolerating " public devotions to the
Blessed Sacrament." The best comment on this
is the passage which I have quoted above from
Mr. Wilfrid Ward. This increasing toleration of
some Catholic practices merely shows that the
Church of England is more and more abandoning
the claim to teach anything definite. And Messrs.
Milner-White and Knox supply abundant evidence that the adoption of such Catholic practices is quite compatible with the abandonment of
some of the most fundamental doctrines of
Catholicism, and indeed of Christianity. " It is
not Pusey and Keble who have triumphed ; it
is rather Stanley and Jowett."

CHAPTER XII

CATHOLIC UNITY

THIS chapter begins by again begging the question. "It is a grave detraction from Rome's claim to have preserved the unity of the Church to mark that the very thing she has not done is to keep the Catholic Church one." Of course, if Eastern schismatics and Anglicans were all really parts of a divided Church, that would be true. But that is precisely what we deny, and what is contrary both to history and to common sense. What has happened is that numbers of Christians have broken off from the Church and formed new churches. But the original Catholic Church founded by Christ does remain one.

Then follows a little more mud-throwing. Accusations are piled up of "persecution, and war, and massacre, and exclusion, and new dogmas, and ceaseless proselytism." It all rather reminds one of the rhetoric of a Bolshevist orator denouncing the wickedness of the "bourgeoisie." So far as it is not mere rhetoric, it is simply a repetition of the charge of persecution, which has been dealt with already. And to say that the Church has "never tried sympathy, nor the answering of just questions, nor a suggestion of common prayer and work " is so exactly contrary to facts that one can only suppose that the writers were in a very bad temper when they wrote it. An immense mass of Catholic writings, from the Encyclicals of Popes downwards, testifies to the sympathy of the Church with all poor souls who are groping in darkness, or in twilight, outside, to her constant endeavours to answer all just questions and to her earnest desire that they should unite with her in common prayer and work, abandoning their man-made sects and submitting themselves to the common Mother of us all.

One question in this outburst of rhetoric is particularly unfortunate. "What help," they ask, "has Rome extended to the persecuted Church in Russia " ? The question evidently expects the answer " None." A very different answer, however, will be given by anyone who took the trouble to read the very beautiful letter of the Holy Father, extracts from which were published in the *Times* of February 10, 1930. I quote from the *Times* report : " The Pope recalls that from the very outset of his Pontificate he made numerous efforts to stop this terrible persecution. At the Conference of Genoa (in 1922) he tried to extract from the Governments represented there a joint proclamation that a preliminary to any

recognition of the Soviet Government should be
' respect of consciences, freedom of religious cults,
and freedom of the goods of the Church.' Unfortunately, these three points, which would have
been particularly advantageous to those ecclesiastical hierarchies unhappily separated from the
Catholic unity, ' were sacrificed to temporal
interests, which would have been safeguarded
better if the various Governments had above all
respected the rights of God, His Kingdom, and
His Justice ' . . . Nevertheless, the Holy Father
recalls his consolation at having rescued the
Patriarch Tikhon, and having saved from famine
and a horrible death 150,000 children, who had
been fed by his envoys until they were com-
pelled to give up their charitable work, because
of those persons ' who preferred to condemn to
death thousands of innocent children rather than
see them nourished by Christian charity' . . .
The Pope then begs Cardinal Pompili to continue the necessary steps for the special Mass
his Holiness intends to celebrate in S Peter's on
the tomb of the Apostle as an act of reparation
against these sacrileges and as an invitation to
the faithful all the world over to make similar
reparation.   He concludes by expressing his
conviction that in this solemn supplication he
will be joined not only by the members of the

Catholic Church, but also by the entire Christian world." (Notice how the Pope here invites non-Catholics to pray with him.)

But now we have to examine the writers' conception of the Church. They reject our idea. What is theirs ? The answer is given in this last chapter, and indeed it is a very curious one, and very difficult to grasp.

" The Church," we are told, " took over, just as we might expect, its view of its own unity from Judaism. The unity of the Jewish faith was founded on *race*. The Jews were an elect, a chosen *people*. This unity was unquestionable and perfectly visible, however widely dispersed in the world Jews might be. It did not depend on government at all. It depended first and foremost on the sense of a calling from God, and secondly on rites of admission and observance which set them apart for this calling, and memorialised the great historical events in it. The new Church, born by the purpose of God in the womb of His older Church, regarded itself at once as a new Israel, a new elect *race* in the world. Its unity indeed was of a higher type than the old ; the bond of blood gave way to the bond of Holy Spirit."

The Jews are manifestly one race, for they are united by the " bond of blood." That is clear enough. But the unity of the Church, we are told, is similar. Only the bond which unites its members is not that of blood, but " the bond of Holy Spirit." If this means anything, it means that all who possess the Holy Spirit are one in Christ. That is perfectly true, but if it is the *only* unity that the Church has, we have got back to the old Protestant idea of an " invisible Church." The unity of the Jews is a visible unity, because the Jews have marked racial characteristics, which make them recognisable anywhere. But possession of the Holy Spirit does not produce such visible outward marks.

Our authors, however, evidently see this. For they have no sooner stated this theory than they at once abandon it, and an attempt is made to show that Roman Catholics, Eastern "Orthodox" and Anglicans form " one race " on entirely different grounds. They are not quite sure whether other Protestants belong to the new race or not. They will not say that they do not. They are content to affirm that the three " communions " named certainly do, leaving the status of the others undecided. This in itself is curious, if the new race is as visible and clearly marked as the Jewish people. In fact, it entirely destroys the theory. For it at once turns out that this new race, unlike the Jews, is not clearly marked and distinguished from the rest of the world, since there are a large number of people about whom it is impossible to say whether they belong to it or not.

However, let us take those who, according to the theory, certainly belong to the new race—Roman Catholics, Eastern "Orthodox" and Anglicans. We have to find some marked characteristics which separate them from the rest of the world and show that they are one "race," just as the Jews are. We are told that all who belong to these bodies are "one in five cardinal characteristics, each one of which is actually more important, more pregnant with significance, than the dreadful fact of their division. Constantinople, Rome and Canterbury are one in faith, one in worship, one in Holy Order, one in fruits, one in outlook and atmosphere."

All this sounds very nice, but unfortunately it is not true, as has been sufficiently pointed out above. It is said that we are one in faith because we have the same creeds. But that is no guarantee of unity of faith, since Anglicans interpret the creeds in a way that is quite different from ours. They reject many dogmas which are not explicitly mentioned in those creeds which they have taken over from us, but which we hold to be essential parts of the Faith.

For example, we regard all the definitions of the
Council of Trent as being essential dogmas of the
Faith. Do all Anglicans agree with us in that .
If not, how can we be said to be one in Faith ?

We are said to have Unity of Worship, because
our sacraments are the same. Here, putting
aside the question of the validity of some Anglican sacraments, I would merely ask whether all
Anglicans are agreed that there are seven sacraments ? And are they all quite clear that they
have got seven ? It is well known that they
hold widely divergent opinions on the matter.

The " Unity of Holy Order " has been sufficiently discussed above. It does not exist, because Anglicans have no true priesthood.

The " Unity of Fruits " has also been discussed. I see no evidence for the claim that the
Eastern " Orthodox " and the " Anglo-Catholics "
are markedly differentiated by their superior
holiness from the old-fashioned Evangelicals.

As for the " Unity of Outlook and Atmosphere,"
it is a very vague phrase, but whatever particular
meaning may be attached to it, it is not at all
evident that anything of the kind exists among
the bodies named, or even among the various
parties and sections in the Church of England itself.

But, in fact, the whole idea of " unity of race "
being the one essential idea of unity found in the

New Testament is entirely contrary to the facts.
It is the old error, common to all heretics, of
seizing upon one truth, or even a single text in
the Bible, interpreting it in their own way, and
shutting their eyes to a dozen other truths and
a hundred other texts, which show their interpretation to be impossible. It is quite true that
S Peter speaks of Christians as " an elect race "
and " a holy nation," but have our friends forgotten all those other texts in which the Church
is spoken of as a kingdom, a household, a body,
and so forth ? Have they forgotten all the arguments by which the older " Anglo-Catholics "
were never tired of showing, as against " Protestants," that the Church founded by Christ was
a definite organised society ?

This, then, is the anti-climax that the Oxford
Movement has now reached. The whole basis of
that Movement was the idea of a teaching Church
founded by Christ. It was on that that they
took their stand, as against the common Protestant doctrine that the Bible was the only
rule of faith, to be interpreted by everyone's
private judgement. Their difficulty always was
to say exactly what they meant by the Church.

One theory after another was shown to be
impossible. Now we have another new one—
this vague idea of a " new race." Some theory

they must have to show that Roman Catholics, "Orthodox" and Anglicans really do form one Church, in spite of appearances to the contrary. And so now, all the others having been tried and found wanting, we have this last despairing effort to show that the proper idea of the Church is that of "one race," and that somehow or other the Roman Catholics, "Orthodox" and Anglicans have certain common characteristics which mark them as certainly members of the "one race," even if it is not quite certain whether the non-episcopal Protestant bodies have them or not. Could there be clearer evidence that the whole "Anglo-Catholic" theory has broken down?

And this is not the whole of the débâcle, for we have already seen that Messrs. Milner-White and Knox have abandoned all idea of a definite truth revealed by God, and handed down from our Lord and the Apostles by a Church with authority to teach. Everybody is left to adopt those doctrines of which he "sees the value," or doctrines are recommended because "Catholic devotion *feels* them to be true."

Now, if these were merely the personal aberrations of Messrs. Milner-White and Knox, they would not be important. The importance of them lies in their indication of the direction in which the "Anglo-Catholic" party is drifting.

It is true that many Anglicans have expressed their dissent and denounced the teaching of " One God and Father of All " in no uncertain tone. We can only thank God that they have. But if they were wiser they would see that this drift of the " Anglo-Catholic " party is inevitable. Some may still stand for the old principles of the Oxford Movement. But the fact is that those principles are worn out. They have been tried and found wanting. That is the chief thing that this book proves. In one way Messrs. Milner-White and Knox are wiser than their Anglican opponents. They at least do see that all attempts to justify the " Anglo-Catholic " position on grounds of reason have failed. They see that all previous attempts by " Anglo-Catholics " to say what they mean by the Church, and to give a reasonable account of it, have failed. They see that, once you deny that the one Catholic and Roman Church is the authoritative Teaching Body founded by Christ, you are driven sooner or later to give up all idea of an authoritative Teaching Body at all. And then finally you are driven to give up the whole idea of definite truth revealed by God. That is why they have taken refuge in this vague subjectivism. They see that there is no other defence of " Anglo-Catholicism " left. What they unhappily do not see is that it is such a very feeble defence, and that by adopting it they surrender the fundamentals of Christianity.

What is the conclusion ? It is very simple. Messrs. Milner-White and Knox have made it clearer than ever that there is only one basis for a reasonable faith. Faith means believing what God has revealed, and we know what God has revealed because He established on earth a teaching Church, one and indivisible, under the Primacy of Peter and his successors. He promised to be with that Church always, and to guide it into all truth, so that it would teach always the truth revealed by Him. That Church has abundant credentials of her Divine mission. Therefore the way to a reasonable faith is to examine those credentials, satisfy yourself that they are sound, and then accept from the Catholic Church the truth revealed by God. There is no other way. Every attempt to find another must end finally in the irrational subjectivism and vagueness of Messrs. Milner-White and Knox. But the promise of Christ has not failed : " Thou art Peter, and on this Rock I will build my Church and the gates of hell shall not prevail against it.